Good luck
and

Best Wishes

Hans Harrey Frish

2018

Use
Your
Head

Lessons of a Lifetime

by

Hans "Harry" Frisch
with
Susan D. Brandenburg

This book was published in the U.S.A. by
Susan the Scribe, Inc.
www.susanthescribe.vpweb.com

Layout and Design:
Philip Barnes
Riverducks Design
riverducksdesign@gmail.com

ISBN: 978-0-9990882-0-3

Table of Contents

Keiner vaist nisht vemens morgn es vet zein.
Nobody knows what tomorrow may bring.

CHAPTER ONE: Vienna, Austria

I was born on July 5, 1923 to Paul and Cornelia "Nellie" Sasvari Frisch, members of a prosperous, prominent family in Vienna, Austria. My brother, Alfred, born January 22, 1922, and I were born in the large house where our parents lived with their extended family at Wein XIII, St. Veitgasse 59. Our home took up a good portion of a city block and our parents resided with us in a roomy apartment on half of the ground floor, the other half housing the home office of our family business, Karl Sasvari Und Sohne, a successful enterprise with offices also in Zurich, Switzerland. Life was good back then ... We had no idea what tomorrow would bring.

Hans as a happy little boy at age 2

On the ground floor of our home, there was a big central salon separating our apartment and the business offices. The salon was a place where the entire family could gather and entertain friends and customers. There was a huge veranda in front of the house, under which were garages, as our family owned several cars. Downstairs in the basement was a kitchen and a place for washing laundry.

Our maternal grandparents, Karl and Julie Sasvari, lived on the second floor with my mother's two single brothers, Otto and Joseph. Everyone in the family was involved in the business, which had to do with branding, creating woven and printed labels, signs and plaques.

Grandparents, Julie and Karl Sasvari

On the third floor of our house lived another brother of my mother, Uncle Richard, and his wife, Netty and their children, Fritz and Gerda. The fourth floor was where our household help lived.

My cousin, Fritz, who was older than Fred and me, had a motorcycle with a sidecar. I remember that we used to ride it around in our back courtyard and have so much fun! On New Years, I recall that we heated lead and put it in water and watch it melt into strange shapes and harden. We loved playing with our cousins in the yard. We all lived so close together, and we thought we would always live that way.

Little did we know what tragedies awaited our family.

We had such an active social life with extended family and friends – traveling often to lakes and resorts on vacations. In the summertime, members of our family would vacation at the resort town of Velden am Wörthersee in the Austrian state of Carinthia, situated at the western shore of Wörthersee Lake.

In addition to swimming in the lake, I remember taking walks to the marketplace early in the morning and eating little fried fish on a stick. Those were happy days. Visitors to the resorts would sometimes pose for group photographs like the one below:

Happy Vacationers at Velden am Wörthersee

My mother had a fourth brother, Armin, who lived in Vienna but not in the big house with us. Armin and his wife, Gertrude, had a daughter, Evy, and they sometimes joined us for vacations.

In 1928, my Grandfather Karl and my Uncle Otto traveled to the United

States aboard the German ship Bremen. Grandfather returned with the impression that people who lived in the United States were "crazy." He said he had never seen people work so hard and the United States was not for us. He later changed his mind.

Grandfather Karl and Uncle Otto

Hans' parents, Cornelia ("Nellie") and Paul Frisch on the driveway of their home.

Paul Frisch

I never knew my paternal grandfather. I only have this old photograph of him:

FALIK SEGAL FRISCH   LEMBERG 1936

I was just nine years old when my father, Paul Frisch, died. My last memory of him was a day when he took me by the hand and we walked to the subway. He wanted to show me off to his friend, but we only got halfway there, and we turned back because he didn't feel well. There was a medical clinic down the street next to the police station. He was taken to the medical clinic and that was the last time I saw him. His death made a huge impact on my life. Even though I was surrounded by loving family, I missed having a father.

My brother and I were now considered half-orphans. There is no denying that the loss of our father was devastating, and it brought us even closer as brothers.

After a time, our mother remarried. Our step-father was Sigmund Rappaport. He went into our family business, working side by side with our mother and her family.

Despite losing our father at an early age, we lived a full, happy life in Vienna, surrounded by friends and family. My brother and I walked to the elementary school we attended, as it was only about two blocks from home. I remember the worst punishment teachers could give me was a note for my parents to sign. I was well-behaved and a good

Hans – Age 9

Fred, Mother and Hans – around 1934

student because it was expected of me by the parents and family I respected.

A famous comedian, Hans Moser, lived in the house right next door to ours. He would talk with me sometimes and always made me laugh with his funny stories. He sort of mumbled when he talked, and made nervous gestures. It was a strange sort of speech and I can still hear it to this day. He was a short man (5'2" tall) and not fat, but he made a big impression by his presence – kind of like our American comedian Jackie Gleason - but not as aggressive.

Hans Moser

Moser and my grandmother had a running disagreement about Moser's big black dog. Sometimes my grandmother would pet the dog and give him treats, and Moser didn't like that.

I vividly remember that Hans Moser used to send me to the tobacco store down the street to buy him three cigarettes – yes, just three – you could buy them individually like that back then. His brand was Sport Cigarettes.

History records that during the Nazi regime, Moser had a big problem with his wife Blanca Hirschler, who was Jewish, but he refused to divorce her. It was only because of his popularity that he was allowed to continue performing. His wife fled to Hungary in 1939 to avoid further trouble and, after the war, the couple reunited. Hans Moser had a long acting career, mostly as a comedian in movies, and died at age 84 in Vienna in 1964.

In addition to the tobacco store where I bought cigarettes for Hans Moser, there were several stores across from our house including the butcher, the deli, and a small sort of convenience store that carried fresh bread and other items, including my favorite chocolate wafers.

Here is a Groschen – the equivalent of a penny.

I needed to save ten of those to buy my chocolate wafers. Today, I order those same delicious chocolate wafers, Manner Schnitte, from Vienna, but they cost quite a bit more than ten Groschens!

When Fred and I got to middle school, we passed all the required tests. There were three versions of middle school available: the one for those who didn't pass the test, one for those who were interested in technology and one for those interested in the medical field. My brother, Alfred, was one year ahead of me and he went into the school for medicine. I chose to go into the technology school.

March 13, 1938, was the day my childhood ended.

Hitler claimed Austria for Germany on that day and was now in complete control of our country. The next morning, when I entered my school, nearly all the teachers were wearing Nazi uniforms. That was my last day of school.

Shortly before Hitler came, our mother's husband had gone to Poland on a business trip and been taken ill. Mother went to visit him and nurse him back to health, so our parents were away from Vienna and unable to return safely to us. I didn't know it at the time, but it would be fifteen years before I saw my mother again. She and our step-father went from Poland to Sweden via Russia and then to Japan and on to the United States, arriving here in 1940. They first lived in New York and someone they knew told them about a motel they could buy in St. Augustine, Florida. They didn't buy the motel because they found they didn't like that business. Another friend told them about a little fish market on Beaver Street in Jacksonville owned by an old Norwegian who wanted to retire, so they bought that.

Hitler took over Austria when I was just 14 years old and my brother, Fred, 16. Our grandparents first sent Fred and me to Berlin where our father's brother lived. They hoped we would be able to get away to another country from Berlin, but unfortunately, no country in the world would take in Jews at that time. After two months, we were sent home to Vienna.

An Ominous Salute ...

My brother and I were back in our childhood home for only a short while before leaving again for Czechoslovakia to escape Hitler. I didn't know it would be the last time I'd see our beautiful big family home until many decades later.

In the meantime, my two uncles, Otto and Joseph, who lived with us in Vienna, were arrested by the Nazis and spent some time in Dachau concentration camp, but my grandparents paid a ransom and got them out. Our family business had an office in Zurich, Switzerland, so my uncles were able to get to Switzerland, but the Swiss would not let them stay because they were Jews. They next went to Nice, France, where they had some connections.

By then, Uncle Otto was married to Olli and their daughter, Ully, was born in France. Otto and his family hid on a farm and escaped the Nazis. Because Otto had been to the U.S. with our grandfather, Karl, he and his family were admitted to the U.S. Our grandparents, also because of the trip that Grandfather Karl and Uncle Otto took in 1928, were able to get a visa and enter the United States. Our grandparents traveled for two days on the Danube to the U.S. Embassy in Belgrade, Yugoslavia to get their visas.

When the Nazis occupied France, it was said that they knocked on doors and gave Jews just ten minutes to gather their belongings. They put them in cattle cars and sent them to Auschwitz Concentration Camp.

For my uncles, Joseph, Armin and Richard Sasvari, the outcome was tragic. Although they were able to hide Richard's daughter, Gerda, on a farm, and she, along with Armin's wife and daughter, Gertrude and Evy, eventually made it to the U.S.A., there was no escape for Joseph, Armin, Richard, Nettie, and my dear cousin, Fritz. All of them perished in the camps, despite desperate efforts by my grandfather, Karl Sasvari, who was in New York writing letters to the U.S. Government and begging for their admittance to the U.S. I recently found one of his letters and it brought tears to my eyes.

Karl Sasvari
254 West 98th St.
New York City

Re:VD 811.111 Sasvari
IVRC Docket No 1647

Gentlemen:

The Department of State,Washington informed me by
letter of June 11,1942 that"a favorable recommendation for the
issuance of a visa may not be sent to the appropriate consular
officer."

Since in reply to my applications of August 2nd and
23rd,1941 I was informed on November 15,1941 that " after careful consideration of the documents submitted,the Department has
given advisory approval to the appropriate American Officer at
Nice for the issuance of immigration visas.",I am induced to
call your attention to the fact that the status of loyalty of
my children to the United States of America has not been changed
by the outbreak of the war between The United States of America
and Germany.

The fact that my children,by chance,were born in
Austria (with the exception of Armin who was born in Cecho-
slowakia) can't be reason enough to call them enemies of the
United Sates of America. I,myself and my children are enemies
of the Germans,that is the reason why we left Austria right-
away after the Germans annexed Austria.

I know that the Department of State uses to consider
persons born in Austria as enemies but I know too that the
Commission can and does grant visas exceptonally and such a
cas worthy of an exception presents itself here. We have never
been Germans and have no reasons to sympatize with them since
by their annexion we lost the greater part of our fortunes and
our existences.

I am 74 and my wife is 77 years of age and it is
only too natural that we would like to be reunited with our
children and their families after years of separation. God
alone knows whether and how many more years are given us to
spend.

It is for these reasons that I appeal to you to
give the case of my children and their families your sympathetic
consideration and to assign to the U.S.Consul at Nice by cable
which I shall pay for the necessary quota numbers thereby
enabling my children to leave for this country in the near
future together with their respective families.

Respectfully yours

Karl Sasvari

I have a book, entitled Memorial to the Jews Deported from France 1942-1944, by Serge Klarsfeld, listing the names of my relatives who died in the Holocaust and that is all I have left of them, except my childhood memories.

I have marked the names of the Sasvari family (Joseph, Armin, Richard, Nettie and Fritz) who perished.

I keep that book in my private office as a reminder of those family members we lost. NEVER AGAIN!

Klarsfeld's most startling opus, pulished in 1978, is a paperbound book, nearly the size of the Manhattan telephone directory, called the "Memorial of the Deportation of Jews of France." It is a listing of more than 80,000 names of Jews deported to the East or killed in France. Each entry includes name, birth date and birth place. The deportees from the main transit camp at Drancy alone came from 37 countries, ranging from France (22,193) and Poland (14,459) to the United States (10) and Tahiti (1). The oldest was 93, the youngest newborn.

It is only by the slenderest chance that the lists of names of the deportees survived. Each passenger list for the 85 convoys sent to the East was typed in four copies. Two went with the convoys and were destroyed, as was the copy kept at the transit camp. But the Germans allowed the Jewish community council in Paris to keep a copy. By the time the Germans fled the city in 1944, the defunct council was forgotten. So were its copies of the lists. When Serge found them in a crate in a French Jewish archive not far from his office, they were faded and crumbling. With a few young volunteers, the Klarsfelds put each page in a plastic folder before attempting to transcribe the names. Sometimes the names were all but illegible, but the team refused to lose a single one.

"These were people who had no graves," explains Serge. "This is the only memorial they may ever have. It shows that they did exist. That is one reason why we have done this. The other is to have a record for the trial. Nazi supporters like to scoff at the figure of six million. Here, from the French side, is the proof."

— from Peter Hellman's profile of Serge and Beate Klarsfeld in The New York Times Magazine, Nov. 4, 1979

I did see my Uncle Otto again only once, when Lilo and I came to the U.S. with our sons in 1953. We spent half a day with him in New York City before heading down to Florida.

Hans Frisch, surrounded by family in front of his Vienna home – a happy past lost forever.

Several years ago, my son, Ben, and I traveled to Austria. I had heard that the family home was rented out as the Embassy of Nigeria after World War II. When we walked up to the house, it looked the same. The outside gate was locked. A man came out to see what we wanted, and I told him, "I was born here." I asked him if my son and I could go in and see the apartment where we lived. The man said, "With pleasure. Give me a minute to get decent." He came back out and showed us the apartment. As I looked around, I felt numb. I was experiencing a part of my past with my son by my side. Ben and I were both speechless. It was as big and beautiful as I remembered – just as I had described it to him all his life. We both stood there silently as I attempted to put together pieces of a happy past life that Hitler destroyed.

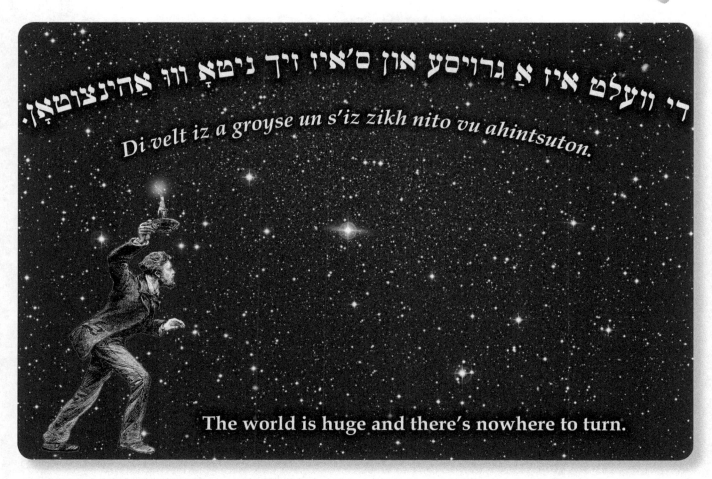

די וועלט איז אַ גרויסע און ס'איז זיך ניטאָ וווּ אַהינצוטאָן.

Di velt iz a groyse un s'iz zikh nito vu ahintsuton.

The world is huge and there's nowhere to turn.

Di velt iz a groyse un s'iz zikh nito vu ahintsuton
The world is huge and there's nowhere to turn. **

CHAPTER TWO: Czechoslovakia

My brother and I were next taken to Bratislava, Czechoslovakia. We went there with our grandparents because our grandfather, Karl Sasvari, had been born in Slovakia, Czechoslovakia.

Alfred and I started out with Polish passports since our father, Paul Frisch, had been born in Poland, but at that time, there was a feud going on between Poland and Czechoslovakia, so every single day, my brother and I had to go to the police headquarters in Bratislava to register our Polish passports.

Again, through our grandparents' influence, we were finally issued Czechoslovakian passports. I remember the day we went to get our Czech passports, the door we walked through was right next to the door of the police headquarters! We were so glad we didn't have to walk through that door any more now that we were Czech citizens! Soon, though, new problems arose, even with our Czech passports. There was nowhere safe!

First, Hitler invaded Sudetenland in Eastern Czechoslovakia and, for a short while, we were afraid he would invade Bratislava next, so we fled to Kosice. Then, after a few days, when that invasion didn't happen, we returned, but we knew it was just temporary – an invasion could happen anytime. We were in great danger and had to get away from there as fast as we could.

We heard of a Jewish organization that would take us by transport to Palestine where we would be able to sneak in illegally at night by walking from the boat through the water to the shore and waiting for the settlers to take us to their settlements, but now, our Czechoslovakian passports had become a liability. My brother and I were at an age where we would be expected to join the Czechoslovakian Army soon. Because he was older and nearer the age for the Army, my brother stayed in Bratislava and I went by myself to Bern and Prague, to acquire the Nansen Passports* we needed to be able to travel to Palestine.

While I was in Prague to acquire these Nansen passports that would declare we were citizens without a country, I was in danger every minute. My native language was German, and the Czechs hated Germans, so I could not ask directions in my native language. Thank God, the French maid in Vienna had taught us to speak her language, so I asked all the

*Nansen passports, officially stateless persons passports, were internationally recognized refugee travel documents, first issued by the League of Nations to stateless refugees. They quickly became known as "Nansen passports" for their promoter, the statesman and polar explorer Fridtjof Nansen.

directions in French and got the passports that allowed us to board a transport on the Danube and eventually escape to freedom.

Looking back, I realize that I was not afraid. At 15, a sense of survival had taken over in my mind. There were no choices left for me or for my brother. The Germans hated Jews and wanted us dead. If we wanted to stay alive, we had to get out.

On March 15, 1939, almost a year to the day after Hitler entered Austria, we were accepted to go by transport illegally from Czechoslovakia to Palestine. My grandmother's sister, Aunt Frieda and her husband, Uncle Phillip, and their two sons, Walter and Otto, were in the same transport on the Danube on a ship that took us to the Black Sea. Hitler occupied Czechoslovakia the same day we escaped. We just made it out in time.

While we eventually made it safely to Palestine, there were many Jews who did not escape from Europe and were annihilated in Nazi concentration camps such as Dachau, Auschwitz, Mauthausen, Natzweiler, Flossenburg, Sachsenhausen, Buchenwald, Ravensbruck, Bergen-Belsen and Theresienstadt, to name just a few.

Theresienstadt was located in German-occupied Czechoslovakia, just north of Prague. It was the camp where we might have been taken had we not escaped. Theresienstadt (Terezin) was presented by the Nazis as a model Jewish settlement during a 1944 Red Cross visit and in a propaganda film, but it was really nothing but a concentration camp. More than 33,000 inmates died as a result of malnutrition, disease and sadistic treatment by their captors. In 1942, it was recorded that 58,491 prisoners were jammed into barracks designed to accommodate 7,000 troops.

**Hans and Fred Frisch – 1939 –
After our escape to Palestine**

Recently, my wife Lilo's youngest sister, Edith, who still lives in Germany, sent me some old "currency" that she found in a suitcase of her mother's. She and her mother had both survived Terezen, though Edith has no memory of it at all because she was a baby at the time.

The currency she found was part of the Nazi propaganda machine to prove to the world that Theresienstadt (Terezin) was a "model camp."

The seven denominations of Terezin currency – 1, 2, 5, 10, 20, 50 and 100 kronen – the krone being the currency of Bohemia and Moravia – differed in size and color from the real thing. Designed in 1942 by Czech artist, poet and inmate Peter Kien (who died in Auschwitz in 1944), the notes featured a vignette of Moses holding the Ten Commandments. Although his original design was approved by the Council of Jewish Elders, the camp commandant Adolf Eichmann, head of the Gestapo for Jewish Affairs, did not approve. Eichmann felt that Moses' appearance was too Aryan and ordered that he should be portrayed with a prominent hook nose and curly hair. Eichmann also commanded that Moses' hand cover

Terezin Currency – 1943-44

the commandment "Thou shalt not kill," and that the denominations be changed from "Ghetto Kronen" to just "Kronen."

Both the back and front of the currency feature a six-sided Star of David, and the words "Quittung Über" (Receipt for), with the denomination in numerals and a warning against counterfeiting. On the back is the signature of Jakob Edelstein, the first Elder of the Jews at Terezin.

The first distribution of the currency was in May 1943 and, although it appeared to be a good means or bolstering the ruse of normality in the camp, the notes had no real economic value but could be used to pay certain taxes, such as those on packages entering the camp. Camp shops were only shop windows and, ironically, those windows were filled with objects seized from the Jews upon their arrival in the ghetto.

The lavish design of the currency belied the actual life endured by the inmates of Terezin. Almost all of the 140,000 Jews that had been transported to Theresienstadt perished, either there or after being transported to Auschwitz. By the time of its liberation on May 8, 1945, only about 17,000 starving and terrorized inmates were found alive.

The currency notes – all uncirculated – are still in good condition, unlike the many inmates who perished in Terezin.

Men antloyft fun regn, bagegnt men hogl.

Run away from rain and you get hail.

מען אַנטלױפֿט
פֿון רעגן,
באַגעגנט מען
האָגל.

Men antloyft fun regn, bagegnt men hogl.
Run away from rain and you get hail.**

CHAPTER THREE: Voyage of the Damned

When the transport down the Danube got us to the Black Sea, we were transferred to the Greek Coal Ship, Agios Nicolaos, for what we thought would be a three-day trip to Palestine. As we sailed through the Dardanelles to the Mediterranean Sea – a narrow passageway with Turkey on both sides – a canvas was put over the ship to mask the fact that 800 illegal passengers were on board.

We had taken enough food for three days and were happy to be on our way, even though we slept uncomfortably in wooden bunkers and were

**Illustration courtesy of Johanna Kovitz, www.yiddishwit.com*

crowded on the ship. Sure enough, three days later we came to the Coast of Palestine.

The plan was for passengers to slip into the water at night and walk to the shore where we would be picked up by people who were working for the Jewish organization, but that plan did not happen.

Instead, a British patrol boat machine-gunned our ship, killing one passenger and wounding several others. There was a British mandate that did not allow illegal immigrants in Palestine and we had been spotted. Our ship ran away from the British patrol boat, getting outside of the three-mile barrier. We made it to the Port of Kea, a small Greek island, but we were not allowed to come into the port. As I said, no country in the world would allow Jews to come ashore.

Somehow, members of the Jewish community in Kea heard about our plight and brought small amounts of food and water out to the boat, but none of the passengers were allowed to disembark.

For four months, we survived on that crowded, filthy ship with almost no food or water. We were given less than 8 ounces of water a day. There was one day when I had dysentery and became so weak that I heard some men discussing whether or not to toss me overboard. Luckily, my brother and I stuck together. We were young and healthy as a result of our upbringing, and we survived. In fact, by the time we finally reached Palestine, we were both hard as a rock.

On July 3, 1939 (two days before my 16th birthday), we hired a small fishing boat and towed it just outside the three-mile zone of the Port of Haifa. Then all of us – hundreds of desperate passengers, piled into that fishing boat. We took a big gamble, all of us crowding into that fishing boat. There were flailing arms and legs everywhere, young people like my brother and me crouching below where the stench of fish and people nearly choked us to death, but we hoped and prayed that the British wouldn't be so cold as to just slaughter us. As we neared the port, the fishing boat began breaking apart and sinking. We jumped and fell into the water, running and swimming for shore and freedom.

Back in 1989, I found an article in the Jewish Journal entitled "Voyage of the Damned." It was about the ordeal we experienced aboard the Greek Coal Ship, Agios Nicolaos, and how survivors Ernest and Edith Rettinger remembered it. The Rettingers wanted to have a 50th anniversary reunion of the "boat people" who were rescued and went on to live productive lives. A photo of the fishing boat, loaded with people, was featured in the article. With the fishing boat breaking up and sinking and

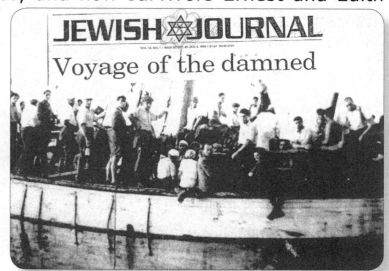

people floundering around in the water, the authorities had no choice but to let us come onto land at the Port of Haifa.

We were held in the quarantine station for three days in Haifa and then released with special permits and sent to a kibbutz in Palestine. My brother and I didn't like the kibbutz – the way it was run was pure communism – everything was owned by everyone, with the old-timers in charge as managers and bosses and the newcomers doing the dirty work. We had been raised in relative affluence in Vienna and this was not an acceptable way of life for us. Alfred and I had vowed that one day we would regain the comfort and prosperity we had been accustomed to as boys.

We only stayed at the kibbutz for a few days and then we headed for Petah-Tikva, a city that was ten miles north of Tel Aviv. Our Aunt Frieda and Uncle Phillip and their sons, Walter and Otto, who had also been on the voyage of the damned and somehow survived, had found a shack in Petah-Tikva and we moved in with them. They had nothing and neither did we, but we were family.

Fred and Hans with their Aunt Frieda

אַ שלעכטער שלום
איז בעסער ווי אַ גוטער קריג.

A shlekhter sholem iz beser vi a guter krig.

A bad peace is better than a good war.

A shlekhter sholem iz beser vi a gutter krig.
A bad peace is better than a good war.**

CHAPTER FOUR: Palestine & Petah-Tikva

My first job was in Tel Aviv at a tire repair place on Hauf Rechov. I still remember the name of the street! It was a ten to fifteen-minute bus-ride from Petah-Tikva. I started out at age 16 with not a penny in my pocket. We called the flat tires "punchers" (punctures).

Before long, I got a job in an auto repair place closer to home in Petah-Tikva called Kachol Velavan (Blue/White – the colors of the Jewish Flag). The owner of the garage was named Jacob Windstrauch. I was walking to work every day from my Aunt and Uncle's house and learning everything

**Illustration courtesy of Johanna Kovitz, www.yiddishwit.com*

I could learn about repairing automobiles. I started out as a helper, sweeping the floor and doing all the menial tasks – watching and waiting and learning how to do it right the first time. I waited impatiently for the day when I would be allowed to hold a wrench in my hand, and when that day came, I felt like king of the mountain! I was elated to be doing productive work.

Cars were scarce and expensive in those days. We learned to work on all types of cars – German, English, French and American – Fords, Chevys, GM Cars, Plymouths, French Citroens – mostly sedans, but some trucks, too … I soon discovered the principle that all automobiles are about the same.

While I was still working at Blue/White, a contracting company by the name of Diskin, which was located in the village of Evy Yehuda, would come in to get their (mostly) Dodge and Studebaker trucks repaired. The British were still in charge then

Young Automobile Mechanics (Hans in center) - approx. 1942

and two things happened simultaneously – a truck driver didn't show up and I offered to drive a truck. I had gotten my driver's license soon after landing in the Port of Haifa. The British Police tested me on a steep decline where I had to shift gears noiselessly or risk losing the chance for my driver's license. I managed to shift gears silently and got my license, so when Diskin needed a truck driver, I was one of the mechanics they asked to drive the truck.

I was once asked to drive a truck to Jaffa, an Arab City next to Tel Aviv. I remember having lunch there from a big wooden bowl in the middle of the table. It was filled with hummus and everybody around the table dipped their pita bread into the same bowl, scooped out the hummus and ate their lunch.

One weekend, I drove a passenger car – a Nash – taking British officers around the country and all the way up north to the Lebanese Border. It was a dangerous, mountainous area where there had been shootings.

Twenty or thirty miles to the north of Petah-Tikva, convoys had gone from the Sea of Galilee through the mountains, carrying American equipment out to the desert – it came by ship into Cairo, Egypt on its way to Russia. If a truck broke down, they would leave it in the deserts and fields and drive on. There were a lot of abandoned vehicles – jeeps and trucks – that could be repaired, have the chassis painted and be resold. Our boss would find the trucks and we'd bring them in to the shop to be repaired. Fred and I helped salvage many of these. We'd have ten jeeps on the line – take them apart and put the pieces back together – clean and paint them. There were some big trucks – water tank trucks with four-wheel drive that could go over any kind of terrain. They were specialty trucks left in the fields. The owner bought them and mounted big water tanks on them for the fire department, along with fire extinguishing equipment.

From the time Fred and I got to Palestine, we were expected to help defend our homes from the Arabs that were all around. It was the duty of every young Jewish man to help, but none of it was official. There were several paramilitary Jewish organizations, the biggest one being the Haganah (meaning The Defense) during the British Mandate of Palestine (1921-48), and it later became the core of the Israel Defense Forces.

The British did not allow Jews to have weapons. If we were caught with even a toy gun in our possession, we were at risk of being thrown into an ancient prison, never to be seen again.

Here is a Magen David Adom "Red Star of David" Emergency Service Team (Hans sitting on the Fire Truck) in about 1947/48

The violence between the Jews and the Arabs was happening every day. The Arabs considered us invaders of their land, never accepting that this was the land promised by God to the Jews for thousands of years. Although I never officially joined any of the paramilitary organizations, there were a few nights when I was among those who went out into the surrounding fields between Petah-Tikva and the outlying village just ten minutes away. We crouched in trenches not much larger than my kitchen counter, three people to a hole. Our weapons were pitiful. I remember that we had one hand grenade, one good Canadian rifle and two lousy Italian rifles. If even one bullet was shot, the commanders of Haganah or whatever group was in charge would demand an explanation for the lost ammunition. It was so precious. Sometimes, in the morning light, a Jewish defender might be found dead in the fields, mutilated and missing limbs, with his ears cut off and his eyes gouged out.

Most of my work in the defense of our homeland was involved in repairing vehicles, teaching others how to repair or drive vehicles – trucks and jeeps – and driving the fire truck or ambulance when needed. There were some nights when I slept at the fire station and was there for an emergency fire run. I also drove an ambulance, volunteering for the Magen David Adom (MDA) "Red Star of David," which was our emergency medical disaster service, similar to the Red Cross. Every male was required to do some duty – we had to go when we were called. Violence had increased greatly by 1947 and so the British government finally decided to withdraw from Palestine. They proposed a Partition Plan to the United Nations to split Palestine into two states, an Arab state (Iraq, Syria, Jordan and Egypt) and a Jewish state, including the City of Jerusalem, giving slightly more than half the land area to the proposed Jewish state. When the UN implemented the Partition Plan, even more violence broke out between the armies of the Arab League and the Jewish state.

Lilo

It was a time of turmoil and trouble, but somehow, I managed to make a living and a life for myself in my new homeland. I even fell in love with a beautiful nurse named Lilo.

I met Lilo at a coffee shop where other people from Vienna regularly gathered. Fred and I would go there every evening and one night, I was introduced to Lilo by mutual friends, Walter and Mela Paskesz, who were from Vienna. Walter and Mela remained friends with Lilo and me for many years, even after they moved to New York.

Lilo was born in the Village of Kurtwitz, Germany on December 13, 1923 to Otto and Anna Senkpiel. She had two sisters, Edith and Gisella, and two brothers, Bubi and Moshe. Sadly, her father and brother, Bubi, fell victim to the Nazis and were never seen again. I met Moshe in Israel and later met Lilo's mother. Her sister, Edith, got married in Germany and still lives there. Gisella (Gissie) lived in Central Florida in a retirement home until she passed away in 2018.

Lilo (whose real name was Lisa Lotta) came to Palestine through Hadassah's agricultural school that she first attended in Germany. She served as a nurse with the British Royal Air Force during WWII in Cairo, Egypt, and came back to Palestine after the war, still working at the British Army Camp.

Lilo - RAF

Fred and I had already made plans to go to the United States and join our mother and step-father in Jacksonville, Florida when I met Lilo, but now things were different. I wanted to get married so I made the decision to stay in Palestine while Fred went ahead with his plans to travel to the U.S. It was the first time in our lives that we had been apart, but my brother had to do what he had to do, and I had to do what I had to do. He left for the United States in late 1947 while Lilo and I were making plans for our marriage.

We were married by a rabbi in a small ceremony with just a few friends present on January 7, 1948. There was no wedding dress for Lilo – there was no honeymoon either, but we were happy. We got married and went right back to work the next day. We looked forward to making a good future together for ourselves and our families.

Hans and Lilo Frisch – January 7, 1948

Apartments were nearly impossible to find, but Lilo had friends and she found one room on the ground floor of a three-bedroom apartment in Petah-Tikva. We immediately moved into Lilo's one room and began our lives together. We shared a bathroom with the other tenants of the apartment

– one family was friendly and the other was not. When the friendly neighbor was done in the bathroom, they would knock on the wall so that we could get in there before the unfriendly ones with two children did.

There was no kitchen available in the apartment, so I took orange crates and built a kitchen by the front steps to the walkway. We had just enough room for a Coleman burner and a wick burner and a couple of pots and pans. Lilo was an excellent cook, but there was little to eat. There were restrictions on food in Israel

Lilo and Hans – Young Marrieds

– we had ration coupons and were allowed about 50 grams of meat and one fish a week per person. Our friendly neighbor bought the meat and we bought the fish and shared – butter and flour were not rationed, but we had basic food – and little of it. Eggplant was one of the vegetables that was plentiful, and there were other fruits and vegetables available.

Across the street from our apartment was a school. Children would drop bits of food on the ground and attract pigeons. Lilo had an idea ... she built a small cage of chicken wire and placed it on top of the flat roof of our apartment. She sprinkled a trail of bread crumbs leading to the cage, propped the door open with a stick and when a pigeon went into the cage, it would be trapped. Then she would pick up the live pigeon and take it to the market so that the Shochet could make it Kosher in the Jewish tradition.

A Shochet is a religious person in good standing with the Jewish community, whose knife cannot have a nick and who knows how to cut the animal with one cut so the animal – which must be perfect with no broken limbs – will not suffer. Women would be nearby in the market plucking feathers of birds (chickens mostly). Lilo's brother, Moshe, lived in a kibbutz and was a bus driver – sometimes he would come by with a live chicken for us.

On May 14, 1948, just five months after we were married, the leaders of the Jewish community in Palestine, led by the future prime minister David Ben-Gurion, declared the establishment of a Jewish state in Eretz-Israel, to be known as the State of Israel.

The British were no longer in charge! We had our own country – Israel – and it felt so good! I drove a jeep in the victory parade on that day!

Now, the Jewish defenders were able to acquire weapons from Czechoslovakia and began to get stronger and more determined than ever. In our hearts, we knew that we would never let what happened to us in the Holocaust happen again. NEVER AGAIN! NEVER AGAIN!

Independence Day Parade – May 14, 1948! Hans driving the jeep full of dignitaries

I did everything I could to support my new wife and soon-to-be born son. I drove a taxicab back and forth from Petah-Tikva to Haifa on Shabbat – when everything was closed and the buses weren't running. I was a "passenger-catcher." I didn't get in the back of the line with the other taxi-cabs and wait for customers … I drove ahead and found people walking and picked them up and took them to their destination. Fred and I never waited for business to come to us – we came to the business!

Our son, Benjamin, was born in the Petah-Tikva Belinson Hospital on November 26, 1948, just ten months after we were married. I was making enough money as an auto mechanic by then, and we were able to move to a larger apartment after Benjamin came.

Our second son, Eldad Karl, was born on June 2, 1952. While Benjamin is a familiar Biblical name, meaning "Son of my right hand," Eldad is an unusual Hebrew name meaning "Messenger of God."

Hans, Ben and Lilo -1949

After working at Blue/White for several years, I started my own business, called Express Garage, with two partners, Itzhak Piven and his son, Matania. We were three automobile mechanics from Blue/White and we discovered that we had enough customers who appreciated the work we did for them that we could break away and build our own business. We were right.

There was a Dr. Belhofsky, for instance, who told everybody, "Harry Frisch is very important to me because he takes care of my car. I could replace my wife, but I could not replace Harry."

During the years that I owned the Express Garage in Petah-Tikva, I was voted into the brotherhood of B'nai B'rith (an organization somewhat akin to Rotary, but more of a true worldwide brotherhood of Jewish men). In order to become a member, another member had to nominate you. Then a secret vote was taken and if you were blackballed by just one member, you could not join. Itzhak Piven, whose uncle worked in the bank, had a brother who was trying to get him in, but he was blackballed. The Pivens were rough and tough. They were natives of Palestine and were called Sabras. Sabra (Hebrew-tzabar) is a tenacious, thorny desert plant known in English as a prickly pear, with a thick skin that conceals a soft, sweet interior. I had learned a lot from the Sabras, especially about defending myself and my village from the Arabs that surrounded us.

Being a member of B'nai B'rith was a benefit for me, as it brought me the respect and business of my brothers in the organization. Before I left for the United States in 1953, the Express Garage was in charge of fixing cars for the Office of the Mayor, judges, and all the top officials of the area. We had a good business and were well-respected for the excellent work we did.

By the time our sons were born, I had achieved a good reputation in Petah-Tikva and my auto repair business was doing well. We had a decent life in Israel, but wanted to go to the United States to be close to my mother and step-father (whom I had not seen for 15 years). We had kept in touch through infrequent letters, and my brother, Fred, had been with them since 1947.

We began to make arrangements to come to the United States, and that, too, was a challenge. In order to get visas, the U.S. Immigration Department required that we have proof of support from a citizen of the United States, guaranteeing that we would not be a burden on society. Mr. Max Blum of Jacksonville signed an Affidavit of Support to be our sponsor. We had to have a Certificate of Good Character, showing that we were not listed as criminals in any police records, and a Certificate of Good Health verifying that we were healthy and did not carry illness.

Lilo, Karl, Ben and Hans – Late 1952

די גאַנצע וועלט איז איין שטאָט.

Di gantse velt iz eyn shtot.

The whole world is one town.

CHAPTER FIVE: Coming to the United States

Karl was a nine-month old toddler in March of 1953 when we left Israel to come to the United States, and Ben was four and one-half. We came on an Israeli passenger ship called the Haifa. It had been sold to Israel by the U.S. We landed in Halifax, Canada, and I remember that we tasted whipped cream for the first time in years. There had been no whipped cream in Palestine! Then we went to New York and spent about one-half day with Uncle Otto (my mother's brother) before coming directly on to Jacksonville to join my brother, Fred, my mother and my step-father.

Illustration courtesy of Johanna Kovitz, www.yiddishwit.com

Nellie, Hans' mother, finally met his sons and wife in Jacksonville.

At first, we lived in a small wooden house at 1022 St. Clair Terrace in Woodstock on the west side of Jacksonville with my mother, step-father and brother. I partnered with two French-Canadian mechanics to open a garage behind the fish market on Beaver Street. They had the equipment we needed, and we all spoke French. As a new garage owner in a new land, I needed to learn some new tricks, so I went to the Jacksonville School of Technology and learned how to work on and repair automatic transmissions. Western Auto brought their customers to me to install rebuilt engines, and after a while, they would not sell rebuilt engines to anybody unless I agreed to install them. Prior to me, about 60% of the rebuilt engines had been returned, but after I started installing them, the returns were almost nil.

Fred had a contractor's license and owned a home improvement business

Frisch Family in Florida

called Frisco Construction, which is still in existence today. He worked out of an office at the fish market, and Lilo was always helpful. She helped my brother with his home improvement business, took care of other peoples' children, and she did whatever she needed to do to help.

The house in Woodstock was quite crowded, so we moved out as quickly as possible, renting a furnished apartment on Silver Street in the Springfield area of Jacksonville, but we weren't there long. There were drugs and prostitution all around us, so we moved again and bought our first home, a two-story duplex on Belmonte Avenue near the Treaty Oak on the Southside of downtown Jacksonville. We rented the downstairs and lived upstairs. I was the yardman, maintenance man, plumber, electrician – everything – but the rent paid our mortgage.

My step-father, Sigmund Rappaport, passed away in 1955 and my brother, Fred, and I had a decision to make. Let me put it this way, I didn't see any future at the garage – three main reasons why: 1) I couldn't find dependable help. When I found a qualified person that knew what he was doing, I couldn't depend on him to come when I needed him. 2) It seemed every customer was broke. They wanted me to fix things I didn't fix, and they didn't want to pay me enough for it. 3) Probably the most important one for deciding to choose to stay with the fish market was that our Mother might have lost it without us. We felt it was too much for her to handle on her own, although she was a strong businesswoman and knew how to treat customers.

One important thing we learned from our mother was how to treat customers. She treated every customer like a sweetheart ... like a good friend who deserved the best. The people she served loved her. She was fondly called "The Fish Lady."

Fred and I always shared in our decisions. We made the decision to go into the fish business full-time together. We vowed, again, as we had in the kibbutz years before, that someday we would achieve the affluence we had enjoyed as boys in Vienna. We incorporated Beaver Street Fisheries in 1955. Prior to that it had been a sole proprietorship with our step-father and our mother working long hours to sell fish in the market.

There was a rule back then (and it still exists today) that you had to be in the United States for five years before you could become a U.S. Citizen. Lilo and I became American citizens in 1958, five years after we came to Jacksonville, Florida. Fred had come in 1947 and was already a citizen by then.

It was probably in about 1962 when we moved from the Belmonte

Avenue duplex. I remember that the boys complained because I-95 had just been built, and the traffic noises distracted them from their school-work. The boys both remember playing beneath the Treaty Oak with friends.

When we moved from Belmonte, I bought a house at 745 Granada Blvd., South on Jacksonville's Southside, where we lived for many years. It was a nice home in a good neighborhood near the St. Johns River. I bought a small 18-foot boat and every Sunday, Lilo would fix a thermos and hot dogs and we'd take the boys fishing.

Use Your Head

46

אין אַ גרױסן טײַך
כאַפּט מען גרױסע פֿיש.

In a groysn taykh khapt men groyse fish.

In a big river you catch big fish.

In a groysn taykh khapt men groyse fish.
In a big river you catch big fish.**

CHAPTER SIX: Beaver Street Fisheries, Inc. — How We Grew

My brother and I figured out one thing right away. Even if people came to the little fish market at Beaver Street 24 hours a day, we could never reach the goal we'd set for ourselves. We had to expand our business.

Every member of our family helped. Our mother, Cornelia (nicknamed "Nellie") took care of the fish market at 2677 West Beaver Street while Fred and I worked to grow the business. Mother had run the fish market completely before we came in. She did everything – cleaned the fish, sold the fish – everything that needed to be done, she did it, while our

**Illustration courtesy of Johanna Kovitz, www.yiddishwit.com*

step father went out and bought the fish. She continued to run the retail market for the remainder of her days, and eventually, Lilo came in to help her run it. Mother passed away at age 77 in 1975 and that is when Lilo officially became "The Fish Lady."

The very beginnings of Beaver Street Fisheries, Inc.

Fred and I began expanding right away, first delivering fish to local restaurants. Sometimes we'd sell as little as five pounds of shrimp or ten pounds of fish filet. Little by little, our delivery business to restaurants grew. When I delivered fish, I noticed that people were calling me Harry instead of Hans. That was okay with me. It was more American.

We soon learned that we could get better prices if we bought more fish at once.For instance, a truckload of fish was much more economical for us than a few fish at a time, but often we could not sell an entire truckload, so we devised a plan to split the purchase of a truckload with our competitors so that we could both profit. That's how we grew quickly from retail to wholesale.

Every Saturday night a truck from South Florida brought in fish at about 11 o'clock. Joe Lang and I unloaded the truck and filled it with Red Snappers from Mayport to sell them to Fulton Fish Market in New York. The New York fish market was ruthless and cold. It was a 24-hour drive to New York and the fish had to get there by midnight on Monday. When the market was good and the fish were on time, all was well. But when the market was bad, if the fish were two minutes late, it was too bad. The buyers in New York found some kind of excuse to reject the fish – they had no scruples.

I remember a man, Jack Yewmans, who had a fish business called Shrimp Exchange on Dennis Street in Jacksonville. He was dealing with the shrimp producers in St. Augustine. He got to New York a little late and was told, "You can take your truckload of shrimp and shove it!" Jack went bankrupt. After that, I was cautious when dealing with the markets in New York.

The first year, we learned a lot about the fish business. I still remember (I've got it written in a composition book), we had sales of $44,000 in 1955. From that, my mother had to make a living, as well as my brother, myself, my wife and two children. We had to pay the mortgage, we had to buy and sell fish. It was not easy, but we were determined to make it.

I didn't know anything about debits or credits back then. The composition book had two columns: "In" (credit) and "Out" (debit). I also noted in some accounts – "We got" and "We owe." There was no accounting department – it was just me!

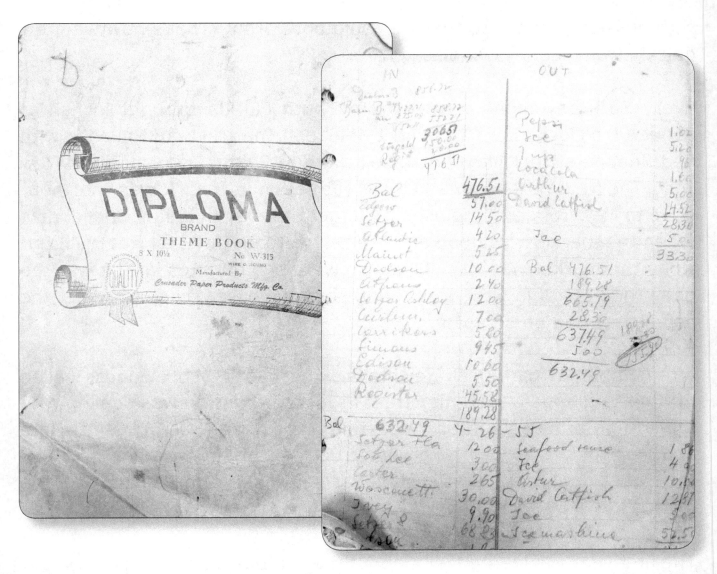

Our days went like this: Fred got on the telephone early in the morning and began calling up different customers to get them to order a delivery two or three hours later.

I got up at 5 a.m. to drive the truck, together with a man named Joe Lang, to New Berlin and Mayport to buy fish and shrimp and then come back to pick up the orders for restaurants.

I spent time on the phone, too, calling customers and potential customers. There was really nothing we didn't do. We bought more trucks and hired a few employees. We continued to grow.

One example of the kind of persistence we had in seeking customers early on was the time I heard my brother on the telephone with the chef at the Ponte Vedra Inn, a resort at the beach near Jacksonville. The chef cussed him out, using all kinds of foul language, and told him to stop calling him every day. He told Fred, "No matter how much you call me, I will never buy fish from you ... Ever!"

Fred was determined. He said, "Let me tell you one thing. I don't care what you say. I don't care what language you're using. As long as you have a telephone over there, I will call you every day for the rest of my life and your life!" There was no caller-I.D. back then, so Fred really did call the man every single day, no matter what!

One day, the chef from the Ponte Vedra Inn called. He said, "Well, you dirty so and so, I need something in an hour. Can you handle it?" He had what he needed in an hour and that particular customer in Ponte Vedra became our best account. Persistence works. You never give up.

In addition to buying fresh fish from Mayport, we began buying fish all the way down state and sometimes we went on Saturday to the West Coast fish houses, where we bought fresh fish to sell the following week. Sunday was the time to fix and repair the trucks so that they could run the next week. That was where my auto mechanic skills came in handy. We didn't have any new trucks, but I knew how to fix the old ones.

Service was always our most important product and word about our service and the excellent quality of all our frozen foods began to get around to local restaurants, but it was as hard to get a regular customer then as it is today.

We never had a 40-hour week here – our values were different at Beaver Street. It was important that we get the most out of our time and money, but we were always fair. Everybody knew that.

Standing in front: Harry Frisch, Nellie Rappaport, Fred Frisch, Earl Darsey, Bill Graham - approx. 1964

Soon, we found out that some restaurants were buying frozen seafood items such as scallops, perch fillets, etc., and since the frozen food people were selling frozen scallops and shrimp, we decided to sell frozen seafood, too.

We first had a freezer that was about eight by ten, and we sold French fries to Milligan's Restaurant, a Jacksonville hamburger chain. We eventually added a thirty-by-forty-foot freezer behind the retail store and built offices on top of it. Having a large freezer made it possible for us to get into buying other frozen foods and that was the beginning of our growth in different products. We also started an additional sales organization in the offices over the new freezer. The name was Frisco Food Sales. After a while, we joined Frosty Acres Co-op and had more buying power. In 1968, we bought Public Quick Freezing Cold Storage, adjacent to the Southeastern offices of the grocery chain, A & P, and built two cold storage buildings. In 1980, we bought the entire A&P complex from N. G. Wade, and Beaver Street Foods came into being.

Frosty Acres

Frosty Acres began in 1954 as a frozen food forum and a food-buying cooperative to lessen the gap between food service distributors, packers and the big chain markets. Beaver Street Fisheries became a member of Frosty Acres back in the early 1970's, increasing our national and international outreach greatly and keeping us aware annually of trends in the food and restaurant business. A big fringe benefit for Lilo and me was the Frosty Acres buying shows and stockholders meetings that took place every year in some of the finest hotels in the USA and abroad. Because of our Frosty Acres connection, Lilo and I traveled to Hawaii, Hong Kong, Europe and took cruises that we would never have taken on our own.

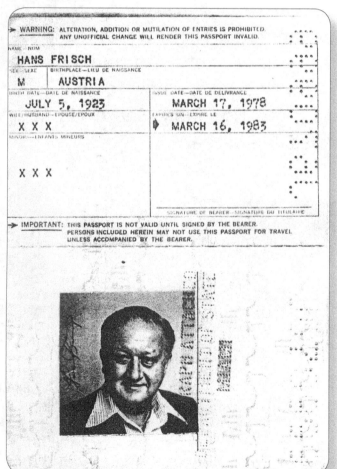

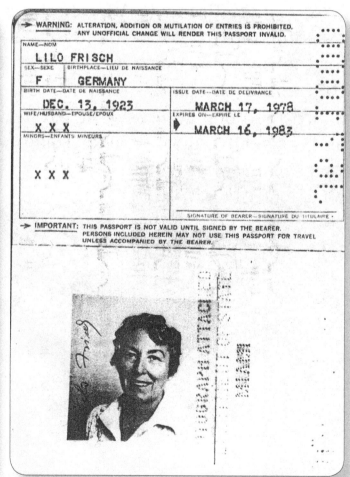

Passports

Many of the formal pictures taken of Lilo and me were taken when we were attending Frosty Acres events.

Another thing besides the travel and benefits of being part of such a large cooperative, I discovered some interesting things about our company. In getting to know others in the food industry, I found out that Beaver Street Fisheries is truly unique. We don't owe one penny to anyone because of our good business practices. We have no money problems. Others in the same industry have law suits on the left and right, but we don't have those problems either. We don't believe in letting a conflict go to court. We sit down and work it out and settle our differences in a civilized manner.

Frosty Acres Brand (F.A.B.) had about 100 small territories with sales meetings all across the United States and the world. These were incentives for the Board of Directors to travel to the finest hotels throughout the U.S. and around the globe. My son, Ben, has taken over for me as a board member at Frosty Acres. Now I'm an Honorary Board Member and, as such, I get fresh Georgia peaches every year.

We had some great times on Frosty Acres trips!

The Defense Logistics Agency, in 1994, decided to use commercial vendors for their food distribution. In addition, they wanted to give our military the same quality (brand) foods that restaurants used. There was a bid out for the Northeast Florida, Southeast Georgia areas, and Beaver Street Foods was proud to be awarded the first Prime Vendor Contract in America.

The wording below is exactly as it appears on the official U.S. Department of Defense website (http://www.defense.gov/conracts).

Contractor: Beaver Street Foods
Department: Defense Logistics Agency
Awarded: 10/20/1994

Beaver Street Foods, Jacksonville, Florida, is being awarded an estimated $8,241,527 firm fixed price contract for the selection of a prime vendor for food and beverage support for Navy customers in Mayport, Florida and Kings Bay, Georgia. This is a one-year contract with two one-year options. Three hundred thirty-five proposals were solicited and 10 were received. Work will be performed in Florida, and is expected to be completed by February 28, 1996. Funds will not expire at the end of the fiscal year. The Defense Personnel Support Center, Philadelphia, Pennsylvania, is the contracting activity (SPO300-95-D-2806).
Total Contract Value: $8,241,527

Prior to winning the bid, Beaver Street Foods had been doing substantial business with the military for years. My son Karl was responsible for the ships and carriers in Mayport as well as the clubs at NAS Jax. Weekly, he would visit the ships in port and make sure we were fulfilling their food needs.

As time progressed, we decided that we should set up a team from

Beaver Street Foods whose total responsibility was serving the military. We hired a former military supply person and surrounded him with other veterans. He built up our military business to include supply bids in Jacksonville and then to supplying Guantanamo Bay in Cuba and all around the region. We were doing great business with the military and when the military decided to upgrade the quality and distribution of food, this is when the bids were distributed. Beaver Street Foods never lost that bid. We maintained it until we sold the business to Sysco Foods in 1997.

Beaver Street Foods always tried to have working relationships with the local sports teams. Karl was a sports enthusiast and enjoyed working with the Suns, the Express, the Bulls and other local sports teams, and it made good business sense to me.

When Karl asked me if he could put a deposit on a suite at the new stadium that had been built in hopes of our getting an NFL Franchise team called the Jacksonville Jaguars, I just laughed and said, "Sure, we won't get a team anyway." This was in 1993 and by 1995, the Jacksonville Jaguars football team began playing in the new stadium and we became the first official food service supplier for the Jaguars. We helped develop the food service and the suite menus, working with the chefs. We had unlimited access to the training, locker and food areas under the stadium. It was a fun and satisfying relationship and we still enjoy our suite at the stadium to this day. In fact, I really look forward to football season these days. Yes, I want the Jaguars to win, but I especially love entertaining people in my suite. It's a great place to meet everyone, from the Mayor to Shad Khan, owner of the Jaguars.

Beaver Street Foods became a leader in working with owners and chefs of the finest restaurants to always help promote our industry. We were extremely active with the Jacksonville Restaurant Association, the

Harry & Fred Frisch

Florida Restaurant Association and the Jacksonville Chefs Association, heavily promoting education in the industry. We provided internships at our company, food for training sessions, and we sponsored dinners to highlight the training of young students. My interest in educating young people was always paramount, regardless of how it was accomplished. I was especially happy to help any industry-specific organization that would promote and help kids get a job in the food industry. I've always been about helping young people get ahead.

Eventually, as we expanded, we opened a meat cutting plant so that we could supply the restaurants with "Center of the Plate," (meat and seafood) – everything they needed. Today, we have HF Outstanding Meat Products – Certified Angus Beef – Top Grade only, for restaurants like the ones at Atlantis in the Bahamas.

There was never a decision made at Beaver Street Fisheries that my brother, Fred, and I did not discuss and agree on it first. Fred had a reputation of being more demanding than I was, but we worked together to achieve our goal of success.

Fred's first priority in life for many years was the business, getting the best price for the best merchandise, but he was gruff and not easy for our customers to deal with. I'd often get calls from suppliers – "Harry, what's wrong with your brother?" It almost became like a game. The supplier would call and complain about the "unreasonable" price Fred was demanding, and I'd calm the supplier down and tell them, "I can pacify him." Pretty soon, we'd be making a deal with the customer that was for a few pennies less than what Fred was demanding, but still profitable for us. Those extra pennies became dollars, but no matter how much you make, you need to stay humble. You can only eat with one spoon at a time. We don't believe in showing off. You can't buy health and happiness with money and possessions. Money is just a yardstick of success.

The years went by and our business grew. My brother, Fred, and I were a team. When we began Beaver Street Fisheries, Inc., Fred worked the outside and did the traveling and bargaining. I worked the inside and ran the business. Fred had the extra push. He was more aggressive. He had the nerve to do things that I would not do. We were together all our lives. We owned everything half and half. I trusted him, and he trusted me. We argued like hell, but we trusted each other.

In the early 1980's, Fred married Bessie Setzer, whose family owned Pic N' Save. Bessie and Fred were a real love-match. Neither of them needed the other's money. They had some good years together, but sadly, Bessie died of stomach cancer. Fred never left her side when she was ill. He truly had a heart of gold underneath his tough exterior, and in spite of the fact that he had a reputation for "firing everyone every day," he would go out of his way to help anybody who needed help.

When Fred died on December 27, 2004, we lost a great man. His obituary follows:

Alfred "Fred" Frisch

FRISCH Alfred "Fred" Frisch, 82, passed away on December 27, 2004. He was born in Vienna, Austria. Following several years in Israel he came to the United States in 1948. In 1950 he made Jacksonville his home. Fred was President of Beaver Street Fisheries and was active in the business until recently when his health interfered. He leaves behind a long list of admiring friends, family, associates and acquaintances. Fred was a member of the Jacksonville Jewish Center, Etz Chaim Synagogue and Beth El Beaches Synagogue. He was predeceased by his wife, Bessie Setzer Frisch. Survivors include his long time companion and friend, Esther Weiss, loving brothers, Hans "Harry" Frisch (Lilo), nephews Benjamin P. Frisch (Pat), and E. Karl Frisch (Missy) as well as numerous cousins, grand nephews and nieces. Pallbearers will be; Abe Bielski, Lathun Brigman, Glenn Pritchard, Leonard Selber, Leonard Setzer, and Charles Trager. Honorary Pallbearers will be; Harold Bloom, Myer Cohen , Dave Dorman, Gene Eberhardt, Jeff Edwards, Ed Fitzgerald, Darrell Glover, and Carlos Sanchez. Funeral services will be held (TODAY), December 29, 2004 at 11AM from the graveside in the New Center Cemetery (43rd & Libert St). In lieu of flowers the family request contributions be made to the Jacksonville Jewish Center, Etz Chaim Synagogue, or Beth El Beaches Synagogue. HARDAGE-GIDDENS Funeral Home, 4115 Hendricks Ave., is in charge of the arrangements. Please Sign the Guestbook @ Jacksonville.com.

Published in the Florida Times-Union on Dec. 29, 2004

עס שיטן זיך פּערל
פֿון זײַן מויל.

Es shitn zikh perl fun zayn moyl.

Pearls flow from his mouth.

Es shitn zikh perl fun zayn moyl.
Pearls flow from his mouth.**

CHAPTER SEVEN: Points of Good Business Practice

If you were to ask me to give a short description or explanation of how we grew our business, I would tell you that the long and the short of it is be honest, be kind, be smart and be diligent.

A few years ago, I was asked to speak to an entrepreneurship class at Jacksonville University. I think the reason they wanted me to speak is due to the longevity of BSF and the consistent impact that this company has had on our community. We employ approximately 400 people – that impacts a lot of lives. And we wouldn't be where we are today without

**Illustration courtesy of Johanna Kovitz, www.yiddishwit.com

all of our employees. The night before my speech, sitting at my kitchen table, I wrote down a list of things that I have used over the years that have helped me to make decisions and I believe set up our company for success. I now call this list the Points of Good Business Practice. What I wrote that night has become a list that is in demand all over the place. People who hear about the list are always asking for a copy of it. I've spoken about it many times since I sat at my kitchen table and wrote it down, and some of the points I wrote need special explanation.

For a man who has only a 7th grade education, I've done well, and I'm proud of my list. My first rule is the one my wife, Lilo, always told me: USE YOUR HEAD!

Here are the Points of Good Business Practice that I wrote out that night.

Points of Good Business Practice:

- **Be Punctual**
  - Don't be late. If you respect someone, you will arrive on time or even early.

- **Set Example**
  - If you want to be a leader, you have to behave in a way you want others to behave. Always do what you say you are going to do. If you are a good role model, others will follow your example.

- **Treat employees with respect**
  - If you want others to treat you with respect, you must treat them with respect. Treat people like people – not like animals. Treat people like family. Why do you think people stay so long at Beaver Street Fisheries? Every person is an important human being.

- **Ethics: Don't lie, steal or cheat**

  Obey the Ten Commandments. I was 9 years old when my father passed away, and when I was 15 years old, I was on my own. I learned that if people get the opportunity, they may give in to temptation. Temptation is a terrible thing. If you have the opportunity to do something and get by with it without getting caught, you may try to do it again and again. Never give in to temptation. I have no regrets. There is a Jewish saying that the end for a thief is the gallows. I deeply believe in God and in following His commandments.

- **Count pennies/dollars**

  Pennies turn into dollars. Whoever doesn't honor the penny isn't worth a dollar. I save the paperclips. Mail comes to my desk and I recycle the paperclips. If I see a penny on the floor, I pick it up.

- **Live (be) humble; not above your means**

  ○ Don't show off. You can only use one spoon at a time. I know what it means to have everything and then to lose it. Hitler came in and threw us out with nothing. We have 400 people working here at Beaver Street Fisheries. I don't want any of them to be jealous.

- **Don't criticize your competitors**

  ○ You're not enhancing your capability by showing how bad the other one is. Politicians try to show how bad the other guy is, and I think that is a way of under-valuing yourself. I always say that we have very good competitors, but there is no room for second best. In everything in life, we try to be the best there is. Winning is important. If the Jaguars lose by one point, they are still losing. We need to compliment our competitors and then outwork them and be the best.

- **Be the best at any price**
  - There is no room for second best. Do what it takes to please the customer. I remember sitting at the stadium with Wayne Weaver, former owner of the Jaguars, and the chef came in and told me, "I've got a big breakfast tomorrow and I need some help." I had someone go to the warehouse at midnight to get what the chef needed. And, speaking of the Jaguars, if they are winning, they are the best, but if they lose by even 2 points, they are losers. There is no room for second best.

- **Every customer is your Sweetheart**
  - The Cloister Hotel on Sea Island is one of the finest hotels anywhere. One lady over there, Mrs. Chapman, needed top of the line service and product and nothing less. We became personal friends with the lady and she actually cried when we sold our food distribution service to Sysco. It was very tough doing business with her. She was determined to keep her chefs happy and we were determined to keep her happy. She maintained a certain standard. We were expected to meet and exceed that standard. She was our Sweetheart. We sent her flowers on her birthday.

- **Pay your bills on time**
  - On my end and on their end – there must be complete trust. Under normal circumstances, there is a line of credit with our suppliers. I would never try to cheat them out of a few dollars. I'm here to service them, with one exception. I don't want to have to call them collecting money. We cannot change the world and from time to time, products get scarce, but the suppliers make sure I have the product because they know

they can set their calendar on getting paid – not early or late – but when the product has been received, a check is written and mailed. Because of that, I have the best credit rating money can buy.

- **Use your head; everything must make sense**
  - Some people have twisted minds – they use excuses and lies, but to me a handshake is worth more than a written contract. Some people are trying to fool me – they come in and think, "He's old – he doesn't know..." They find out differently. Sooner or later, when someone tries to take advantage of you, they make a mistake. Don't cheat. Be careful. We will learn their tricks. Life is difficult, especially for dishonest people. The product delivered, and the money collected have to make sense – some drivers have been dishonest – we find out and face him with it and fire him.

- **Possibly, work earlier for someone in the same field**
  - Know the pitfalls and problems of the job so that you are prepared. You can't learn the business in college – you need to be in the field, learning from the experts. The only type of person I hesitate to hire is a college graduate – very often, college graduates think they know more than the man in the warehouse, but the man in the warehouse knows more than they do about that particular job and they need to learn from him.

- **Don't make commitments or promises unless you are absolutely sure you can deliver**
  - Your reputation depends on you being able to deliver on your promises. If you can't deliver on your promises, people won't trust you.

- **Sometimes tell people "I Need Your Help."**
  - We lived for 15 years in Palestine where everyone was Jewish and we never went to the synagogue, but when we came here, my thinking was different. I didn't have the religious education or deep commitment to keep a Kosher home, but I wanted my sons to have a choice. There were three kinds of synagogues here – Reform, Conservative and Orthodox. Etz Chaim, the Orthodox Synagogue welcomed us warmly. I needed help and I asked for it and they gave it to me. They are still my synagogue and I support them generously to this day. Don't be afraid to ask for help.

- **As an employee, volunteer for projects no one else wants and show you can do it**
  - Always go above and beyond. That might be the job you were meant to do and when you learn how to do it, you might be cementing your future in the company.

- **If necessary, go out of your way to make a friend**
  - We've all got to have friends. Friends help each other, and we all need help once in a while.

- **Smile constantly**
  - Nobody likes to talk to a sourpuss. It's easier to smile than to frown, anyway, and people will feel more comfortable in your presence. Example: If you have two deli's side by side – both with the same product and the same prices – but one has service with a smile and the other doesn't – which one will you always go to?

- **Figure out (know) what you don't know**
  - When I meet people that know more than I do about a certain

thing, I observe them and try to learn as much as they know. I don't exactly pump them for information, but I'm not afraid to ask questions.

- **Place must be clean, neat and pleasant**
  - Cleanliness is next to Godliness. If everything is clean and neat and pleasant, people are happier to be there.

- **Respect**
  - Again, respect others and they will respect you.

- **Give back**
  - God gave me so much, I want to give back to others as much as I can.

- **Keep old people**
  - If he or she wants to work, he or she can work with us until their last day. An old person has the wisdom, know-how and judgment of two young people - it cannot be matched. It's just good business to keep the old people.

- **Let them leave**
  - When an employee comes to you and tells you that they have a better opportunity elsewhere, you need to let them leave. In fact, you need to make yourself available to help them leave. I tell them, "I hate to lose you as an employee, but I don't want to lose your friendship. If I can help you get this position, I will." That doesn't mean they can't come back. If you try to make someone stay by paying them a few dollars more, they will always wonder what might have happened if they had gone. By trying to keep someone from advancing, you are stealing their soul. By letting them leave, you are

releasing them to return once they discover the grass is not greener elsewhere. Some of my best employees are the ones who left and came back. They call me and say, "Can I have my job back?" They know I had their best interest at heart and they know the grass isn't greener after all. Today, without those people we wouldn't be as successful as we are. They are some of the best employees we have.

- **Truth is the best lie**
  - Whoever lies once will lie again. Never start lying and you'll never have to remember what you lied about.

- **Communication**
  - Communication is give and take – listen and talk – hear and learn.

- **2 people on everything**
  - Always have two people on every project. I never did anything without asking my brother his opinion. I have two people view every document, every piece of paper, every product. Check and verify. When you have two people, the chance of making a mistake is cut down by 50%.

- **2 night's sleep**
  - When I have a decision to make, I sleep on it for two nights and that helps me avoid making decisions on impulse and emotion. I don't make many decisions without two nights sleep. If I still think it's a good decision after sleeping on it for two nights, then it probably is a good one.

- **Impulse and emotions**
  - When you let impulse and emotions rule, you are giving into

temptation – not a good thing. If you are thinking, I want it, I gotta have it, cut that out – think about it for two nights – if it's meant to be, it's meant to be.

- **Learn to like what you have to**
  - Learn to like what you have to ... if you cannot learn to like it, get out of it. You cannot be the best if you don't like it. You might do the job, but you'll never excel if you don't like it.

- **Privileges and obligation**
  - Life is like marriage – you have certain obligations and you are entitled to certain privileges. You need to balance the scales somewhere in the middle – give as much as you get.

  - Any time you chop wood, there are some chips coming off. If you have vision and common sense and your heart's in the right place, you will be able to balance the privileges and obligations well. The cream always comes to the top.

- **USE YOUR HEAD**
  - This encompasses all of the Points of Good Business and even more!

- **Ask yourself these three questions:**
  - How did it happen?

  - How do we correct it?

  - What do we do to make sure it doesn't happen again?

I always say that anything I've got is for sale if the price is right, with one exception – it cannot affect my night's sleep. I tell all my friends that if they need an explanation about my Points of Business Practice, please call me. As usual, I'm available 24/7.

Naches fun kinder iz mer tei- er far gelt.
Joy from children is more precious than money.

Harry, Lilo and Grandchildren

CHAPTER EIGHT: Children and Grandchildren

Our whole family worked at Beaver Street Fisheries, first located at 2677 West Beaver Street. Mother, Fred, Lilo, Ben and Karl and I worked here, and each of our grandchildren worked here, too. It was and is truly a family business, just as Karl Sasvari Und Sohne was a family business back in Vienna where Fred and I were born. We worked long hours each day – and after many years, we achieved our goal and we did it without lying, stealing or cheating. It is in our blood, and I could not have asked God for a better family.

Harry, Karl and Ben Frisch at Beaver Street Fisheries - 2015

I want the future generations of the Frisch family and all of the people we employ at Beaver Street Fisheries to take my Points of Good Business to heart. I also want them to live by the Ten Commandments that God gave to Moses and that are still valid and important today. In fact, they could have been written last week instead of thousands of years ago!

Lilo and I were blessed with five grandchildren and three great-grandchildren, so our future generations are assured. When our sons, Ben and Karl, were growing up, Lilo did most of the raising because I was so busy with work, and I'm grateful that she did such a fine job. I could not wish for two more loving and wonderful sons than Ben and Karl Frisch.

Ben Frisch

My father was the best auto mechanic in Jacksonville

Looking back at my boyhood, I remember watching Pop work on cars. My father was the best auto mechanic in Jacksonville and I have always been mechanically inclined, probably from watching him from such an early age.

I think for this reason I've been a car enthusiast most of my life. I've bought older cars and tinkered with them for years. The first car I ever drove was Dad's 1954 Chevy – I was about 12 or 13 at the time. My first car was a 1958 green Volkswagen.

I still love fast cars and I believe that if you can't take care of something, don't have it.

Ben, 3 – driving a toy jeep

In 2008, the cover of one of the industry magazines had a photograph of a Dodge Challenger, Chevy Camaro and a Ford Mustang and the headline read "Rebirth of American Muscle."

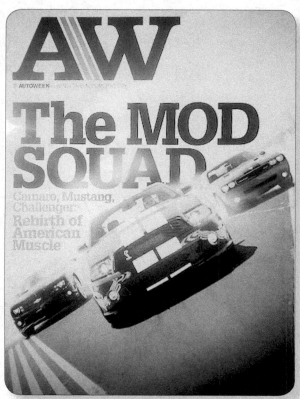

That dramatic cover changed my life. Now I've got all three of those cars!

I buy a lot of cars for the business over in the Bahamas – we have over 100 vehicles – 50 cars and 50 trucks, and 300 people working over there. I always bought Fords for all my people. Fords were easy to fix in the Bahamas. I shipped over all my father's and uncle's cars after they were a few years old.

I spend at least half of my time in the Bahamas, and that

is due to my Uncle Fred's foresight in wanting to buy a business over there. It has been a great thing for me and for our company, although Pop didn't see the big picture of it at first.

Karl, Pop, me and Uncle Fred - approx. 1954

Looking back, my Pop and Uncle Fred were like night and day, but we all knew both of them had hearts of gold. Where Pop was friendly and pleasant, Fred was aggressive and gruff. He would never hesitate to call people names. Where Fred was often harsh, Pop was kind. People respected them both, but they usually liked Pop better than Fred.

Pop believed in giving credit where credit was due. Both of them were hard workers, always, and determined to succeed. I think I took a little bit from each of them. I don't always say it was my idea and I think it's important to try to understand other people's problems when you're working with them.

Fred was a great negotiator. He loved to travel and spent a lot of time in Mexico and South America – spoke fluent Spanish. He was a hard worker. He saw no difference between weekdays and weekends – he worked constantly.

In 1969, while at the University of Florida in the Advanced

Air Force ROTC, in lieu of going into flight training after I passed the test, I opted to go into the family business. I wanted to fly but felt that the family business was not only doing well but it was good enough for my family so it was good enough for me. And I knew that given time and training, I would have a lot to contribute to helping it grow. I made the right decision. I did sign up for the reserves and was lucky to be assigned to the 3396th Reception Station in Gainesville in May of 1969. I served in the Army Reserves for six years – a weekend every month, from Friday to Sunday, and two weeks of active duty every year. It paid $300 per weekend, which was good money back then.

I graduated from the University of Florida in June of 1971 and by August, I was working in the Bahamas. I did some traveling with Fred and enjoyed it. Fred had a Bahamian acquaintance, Mr. Heastie, who had a small lobster plant in Nassau. We bought lobster from him and ended up buying the plant in 1971. That's when I went over to work in the Bahamas the first time. We had eight people in Nassau at the small lobster plant and were upgrading it constantly.

In 1972, Pop sent another guy over to the Bahamas and I came back and worked for a year at Beaver Street, but the Bahamians were cliquish and didn't take well to outsiders and that guy didn't last. They liked me, so I ended up working there and selling here – going back and forth, which I still do to this day.

In 1973, we bought a small ice-plant and a little warehouse. I got to know the people and they got to know me. We started growing on our own, going out and selling food to restaurants, and we became a seafood distributor in Nassau. We bought a few more acres of land and continued expanding. Mr. Heastie was almost like a father to me over there – he made me get up every morning before the sun came up. It was a pretty tough place

Lilo, Ben and Pat – About 1973 or 1974

back then. I had a girlfriend, Pat, who moved to Nassau and helped me. Pat and I eventually got married. She handled the money over there – sometimes we'd have as much as $20,000 to $30,000 cash – everything was done in cash. We had to be cautious – nothing was simple over there. I don't know if I would have been able to do it without Pat's help.

By 1997, we had built it up to $40 Million in sales. There was no more room to grow. Our food distribution included more than 2,000 items. That year, the European Union inspected our plant and found that it didn't conform to their regulations because there wasn't enough space. We had a competitor in the produce business who was starting to get into our food distribution business as well.

I decided we needed to build a new facility for food and produce *and seafood. My uncle did not agree. He told me, "You've got the brains of a dog!" That didn't stop me. I went ahead and built it against my uncle's will. In June of 1998, I bought 112 acres of land in an undeveloped part of the island and built a state of the art plant. Jeff Edwards helped with the design of it. I wanted it to look like Sysco on Riviera Beach – like a U.S.-built plant – and it does. It's built like a fortress – 300,000 square feet.*

Our Bahamas Facility

I subdivided the land and the building. We had Tropic Seafood and Bahamas Food Service – dry warehouses and freezers. We had 16 million pounds of food in the freezers. In 2013, we sold Bahamas Food Service to Sysco. We had to get the approval of the Bahamian Government – it took nearly three years for the Prime Minister to approve of an American Company coming into the Bahamas. I continued to run it until 2016. We went from $40 Million to selling $200M, and even after selling it, I grew the company 20%.

Now I run Tropic Seafood only, and I am looking to grow it but don't know in which direction. I am nearly 70 and should probably be slowing down, but I love the business and I don't know if I'll ever stop trying to grow it.

Fred loved the business, too. He taught me a lot. He never gave me a compliment – no matter what – but he didn't compliment anyone. He didn't try to be well-liked, either. We had a plant we worked with in the Abaco Islands and they were good people, honest and church-going, but they couldn't get along with Fred. For years, he and this man, Gurth Russell, fought tooth and nail over every negotiation. In 1999, I took over everything, including the relationships. It was a win-win. Mr. Russell, talking about Uncle Fred, told me, "That man was impossible to work with!" We've worked together for twenty years – and now he works exclusively with us – no contract, just word of mouth. We trust each other and there are many thousands of pounds of lobster involved.

I'm supposed to be doing things differently now that I'm almost 70, but I still spend more than 50% of my time in the Bahamas. I'm constantly thinking about growing the business. We sell live lobsters from Nassau to China – it's global and exciting. I've always put business before my personal life. I like doing the deals.

Glenn Pritchard is my man in the Bahamas – Jeff Edwards has also helped me a lot in the Bahamas, especially when I was building the new plant. Jeff is a detail man – also mechanically inclined, like me.

Pop is a great role model. I've learned so much from him about respecting people – treating people right. I've never met anyone who didn't like him. He has a way of getting problems solved. He is very intelligent – has so much common sense. I love him. We talk every day.

Among other things, I learned from Pop that it either happens on its own or you make it happen. Our foundation helps people, but we've always helped people. We're involved in a lot of organizations that make a difference.

I don't remember much about my grandmother. We called her Umama. I remember that she smoked a lot. She was married to a man named Rappaport.

Even before my grandmother died, Mom went in to work at the Fish market. They called her the fish lady at work. I remember as a boy, selling fish at the market – it was five people deep in there. My friend, Chuck Newcomer, and I went there to work after school. There was a big man named Mr. Gibney who worked there with my mother. I must have

***Umama with me
and Karl – around 1955***

been in about 11th grade at the time because I remember him yelling, "Look Alive in '65! Stack 'em high and sell 'em cheap!"

We'd sell pounds of fish – gut them and filet them and put them out for display. We were wet in there all day – the whole place was damp and humid and soaking wet. I remember that, early on, Umama was back in the back looking out the window, and Mom worked the register at the counter.

Mom was a working mother. Her first priority was the family and business. She was very smart – a good wife to Pop and a good mother to Karl and me. When we were growing up, we could not afford what other people had. Even when we got better able to afford things, we were always under the radar. We never showed off. While other people were out enjoying themselves, *we were usually working, although we occasionally got a chance to relax on a weekend and enjoy simple pleasures like going to the beach.*

Mom with Karl and me at the beach.

My mother was a great cook. Nobody made chicken soup like my mother. Her baked chicken was delicious, and she was famous for her brisket. She made great desserts too – sour cream pound cake. She made only nutritious food. She made Gefilte Fish – from ancient days it's been part of Jewish life. She used carp for the Gefilte Fish– which was considered trash fish, but she deboned it and cooked it into a patty – like a flat football – on every Jewish holiday. It was a laborious task that took her two days, but everybody did it for holidays. When carp was not available, she used red bass and mullet (two other inexpensive fish varieties). Her Gefilte Fish was delicious. She always put a slice of carrot on top and served it on green lettuce. The presentation was important, too.

When we lived on Granada, Mom was always out in her garden. There was damp, good soil, nutrient rich on our land and she grew everything in it – tomatoes, corn, cucumbers, greens, etc. Pat learned to love gardening from Mom. Mom always said we would never go hungry if we had something growing in our yard. Pat learned that from her and still has citrus or vegetables growing to this day.

In my life, time is of the essence. I work my day around the time factor. Even when the time changes, I make sure all my clocks are changed the night before.

I went to Vienna with Pop in 2009 – to the home where he was born. I felt happy for him when we walked through – it was emotional. We went to see his father's grave and visited with his cousin and his cousin's son. My grandfather's signature, on the tombstone, was remarkably like that of uncle Fred's.

Pat and I have three fine sons, Adam, Mark and Steven – all of whom are doing a good job in the family business. Pat did most of the raising of them because I was out of the country so much. We made sure they had a good Jewish upbringing. My passion for business took me away and I lost a lot of weekends with the boys. Pat's parents moved to St. Augustine and were active with the boys when they were growing up. My parents were working most of the time.

Today, I'm still so busy with work that I don't even have time to read my favorite magazine, *Business Week*. But I always have time to call Pop. I need to hear his voice every night, and he needs to hear mine.

On their 60th wedding anniversary, we had a dinner party for them and bought them a wedding cake – something they didn't have when they got married. Pat wrote a beautiful poem about them and presented it to them.

* * * * *

It takes two special people,
To make a loving pair.
Tonight your familiy is around you,
A special evening to share.

I can't believe it's been sixty years,
Sixty years ago you were wed.
And now I have some thoughts on my mind,
There's a few heartfelt words that need to be said.

Firstly, I just want to say thank you,
I'd like to thank you for all that you have done.
For your love, understanding and support,
And many many thanks for giving me your son.

I also know life wasn't always easy,
You both struggled and worked hard along the way.
But you never let that get you down,
And you are a true success story today.

Mom, you babysat, you worked, you cooked,
You made a house a home.
You raised two sons while Pop worked hard,
An unconditional love is what you've shown.

Pop, you've been a hard worker all you life,
Determination is a quality you have never lacked.
Quite amazing really is the perseverance you have,
Pushing ahead, moving forward and never looking back.

A successful, thriving business is what we have today,
Truly a dream come true.
For all your early mornings and late nights,
We owe our thanks to you.

You are a perfect couple,
In a marriage that is blessed.
May your love shine like a beacon,
A guide for all the rest.

To a couple who brings joy to all,
May happiness surround you two.
May your love continue warm and bright,
That is what I wish for you.

Happy 60th Anniversary,
That's what this evening's for.
Here's to you Mom and Pop, you're wonderful,
And here's to at least another sixty more.

I Love You,
Pat

January 19, 2008 – Dinner at Epping Forest Yacht Club

Karl Frisch
Everyone loved mom's weiner-schnitzel

In my childhood, my mother always was home. She worked retail after my grandmother got older, and she was gone in the afternoons sometimes, but I remember her at home in the kitchen.

We called my grandmother Umama – German for grandmother. We'd go to Umama's house for dinners – I remember cucumber and tomato salad with oil and vinegar. She lived on Serenac behind Beaver Street at first and later moved to Hendricks Avenue. I lived in that same house on Hendricks for a while.

**Pop, me and Umama
- about 1953**

Growing up, we worked at the fish market Saturdays, and during the summers, scaling fish, fileting fish – doing whatever needed to be done. Everybody started at the bottom. We were never given special treatment.

Mom was a hard worker. She was way ahead of her time when it came to the fresh (organic-type) foods. She cooked everything from scratch. She would go to Hall's Poultry off of Myrtle Avenue and have them slaughter the chicken there – pull out the feathers but keep the feet. She wanted the soup. Fresh – always fresh. I don't remember canned goods, or her ever using cake mix – that's why I am a foodie. Everything she made was healthy – she grew vegetables and fruit in the yard. She had all the trees and vines. I can picture her working in the garden. She would send me to A&P in San Marco for bones to make soup. In those days, the butchers would give you the bones free. Her soups were always delicious. Knowing her, she probably used the least expensive meat to make it good, and everything she made was good.

The favorite thing for everyone was her Weiner Schnitzel (veal, pounded thin, dipped in egg and cracker meal, garlic and seasonings and fried). Briefly, you take the veal out of the pan after it's cooked and brown the potatoes and red cabbage in small pieces. Serve it all on homemade noodles with a little sugar. Homemade noodles! She also made the best chicken soup. One of her secrets was that she used hot water over the chicken rather than cold. It got more of the fat out. She put in carrots and celery and she always said if you want your soup to be darker, put in some onion skin. That will turn it darker.

She and my father both – from Germany and Austria – believed in the idiom, not by strength but by brain - Nicht bier moach but koach. I've heard that all my life.

I was just going through her cabinet the other day and thinking that it's easy to have the right tool when you cook – always from scratch. She the right tools and she also had an old green German recipe book. I wish that ten years ago that we had recorded her recipes and more – recorded her voice. She called me Mukelah … that's what she always used to call me. I don't know what it means, exactly, but Pop says it's a term of endearment.

In our house on Belmonte, we had a kerosene stove in the middle of the house – temperatures were colder in those days, only getting up to the 60's and 70's. Sometimes there would be frost on the roof. We would put pillows on the heater and run and get in bed.

We always ate a lot of fish – fish heads and chicken feet for soup. Mom used to say, "Never talk when you're eating fish – you can't tell if all the bones are out."

At home, she never cooked bacon or ham, but when we

vacationed at the Chateau Motel on Collins Avenue in Miami, an efficiency with a kitchen in it ... we would always cook bacon.

My parents were not Kosher. They were spiritual – not religious, but their support of the Synagogue was unbelievable. Bingo Wednesdays and Sundays – Etz Chaim on University Blvd. – bingo hall – behind synagogue. Loaded with smoke – everybody smoked back then – she would come home reeking of smoke – somebody needed to be there, so she went. She cared about the synagogue.

We attended Etz Chaim when we were a young family. They welcomed us warmly. It's an orthodox synagogue but they were the ones that wanted us to come. We had Hebrew School after school.

I played drums in a John Gorrie summer program once. I went to Southside Grammar School – 1st through 7th – and then Florida Military School in Deland. They wanted us to learn to be on our own – learn that we had to do our own things - fold clothes, polish shoes, make beds. I graduated from Wolfson in 1970 and, attended University of South Carolina and then went into the family business.

While in college, I did what I could to make extra money. In the apartment complexes, I'd run the activities room. Beaver Street sent meat and I made and sold sandwiches. I also worked as a painter – painting ceilings of spas with black paint – cabinets at apartment complexes – sprayed, varnished, sanded, and painted them again. I always learned to do whatever I did to the best of my ability. Whatever you do, do it right – be proud of your work.

Pop would leave before I got up to go to school and get home when I was going to bed or doing my homework. He worked 6 ½ days a week at least, and nearly that much even when we were on vacation. For instance, on the way to Miami for vacation, we would take a full day driving. He stopped at every single fish house to talk business. We'd sit in the car and wait while he went in and talked.

Occasionally, we would go to North Carolina – to a little lodge in the Smoky Mountains for a week. We'd drive to Chimney Rock and Sliding Rock. If there had been a cell phone, Pop would have been on it, but as far as I can remember, he actually did have some relaxation when we were on vacation in the Carolinas.

Mom and me on vacation in NC - around 1958-1959

When we were young, Pop would take us fishing on Sundays. We'd go the Devil's Elbow Fish Camp at Matanzas – catch flounder, whiting, sometimes red bass. We'd rent a little boat and spend all day out there. Mom would fix sandwiches for us and come along. She loved to fish, too, and we all loved those days. Later, he bought a boat and it wasn't quite as much fun to fish. The boat had to be cleaned – not later, but Now!

One of my father's favorite sayings is that Truth is the best lie – then you don't have to remember what you told somebody.

Mom taught me how to iron, wash clothes – helped make me self-sufficient. I sewed buttons on for the kids – my mother taught me all that – she always wanted me to learn to play an *instrument – make money by playing something, but I never learned.*

Whenever we were sick – she was infamous for giving us honey and whiskey as a cough syrup – it's one of the reasons I don't drink today. We would have to go stand on top of a step stool by the stove. She'd have a pot on the stove with toothpicks in the boiling water, moving around like little boats. We'd have a towel over our head so we could take in the steam – she called the toothpicks boats. I think they were there to distract us.

If you walked into the freezer at the fish market everything had better be straight – and clean – no paper, dirt – nothing on the floor – cleanliness is next to Godliness is what Dad always says.

Rotate the product – older on the top – newer on the bottom – detail oriented – color coded – know the color – Pop had no problem cussing you out. He was good with a belt – no problem hitting you (never abusive). There was no talking back to my mother – she would say, "Wait until your father gets home." His belt was the definite "behavior corrector." He would fold it up and spank. I don't remember Mom ever spanking me. She left it up to my father.

The main rules: Never lie, cheat or steal.

At five years old, I was working at Beaver Street. I'd go with my father. I'd take the hook and try to pull 100-pound boxes of fish into the cooler. I remember standing on a Coca Cola Crate next to my grandmother while she was selling fish. She had an old-time scale for weighing the fish. I would go there after school – work Friday nights, when my father had all the ice taken out and the freezers cleaned. The fish were turned, the ice was clean and fresh. When you walked into the fish market, you did not smell fish – it was that clean. I worked in the freezer for a while, and as a truck driver. It was stick shift and the Acosta Bridge was steep – a challenge to negotiate with a full truck.

We never had customers – everybody is a friend. You do business with friends, not customers. Never had answering machines at Beaver Street. Personal service was first and foremost. We had more blacks than whites in our employ – my father doesn't have an ounce of prejudice in him. He cares about everybody. People are people.

My philosophy: Treat every day like it's the last day of your life. You never know. Don't worry about things until you have a reason to worry. I had a heart attack on October 20th 2005. It was six a.m. and I was at work, bringing my briefcase upstairs with my newspaper. I took a Tums, but still had terrible pain. I drove to St. Luke's on Belfort Road. I was in the emergency room and I called Dr. Willis and said, "I think I'm having a heart attack – I'm in the emergency room at St. Luke's." I'd just been at a food show in Las Vegas – had been out of breath and not feeling good. After I called Dr. Willis, they took me right in. It was about 11 a.m. and I looked out of the Plexiglas window and thought everybody's gone – what's happening. I asked the nurse where the doctors were, and she said, "They're out talking to your family." That was a strange feeling. Turned out I had clogged arteries – including what they call "the widow-maker." I had two more stints after that. Used to go to the gym five days a week.

My son's Bar Mitzvah was a circus, literally. We had the FSU Flying Circus at Jacksonville Country Day School – under a big top – everything Kosher – 350 people – people still talk about it. It was unique. Recently, it was the 20th anniversary of Daniel's Bar Mitzvah – he called to talk about it and joked that he's still upset because he never got to taste all the food!

My daughter, Erin's Bat Mitzvah was a Luau, with superb first-class Hawaiian entertainment and a Luau food buffet which overwhelmed everyone in attendance. Hers was a unique and exciting Bat Mitzvah that people also still remember.

Pop, Daniel and me

Mom, Erin and me

I'm now retired, still involved as an investor, and live part-time in Hawaii, but I try to be here whenever he receives an award or honor of some kind, which is very often lately.

Pop is so popular, there's a joke that goes: When a picture was taken of my father talking with Pope Francis, someone looked at it and asked, "Who's that guy standing next to Harry Frisch?"

* * * * *

Ben and his wife, Pat, gave us three fine grandsons, Adam, Mark and Steven, all of whom are top executives now at Beaver Street Fisheries! Karl and his first wife, Michelle, gave us our grandson, Daniel, and our only granddaughter, Erin, both of them quite successful in their chosen professions. When our grandchildren were growing up, Lilo and I stressed to each of them that they were privileged to live in a family of means, but they must always rely on their brains and their character, because wealth can be taken away in an instant. I always checked their report cards from school and rewarded them for using their brains. Lilo and I reminded them often to use their heads, and value what they had because they might not have it forever.

Harry - gold watches

When my brother, Fred, and I left Vienna, we took with us only two remnants of our former affluence – Fred had our father's gold watch and I had my gold Bar Mitzvah watch. Back in those days, every pair of pants had a watch-pocket, so these were both pocket watches. Those watches were shining symbols to us of the life we left behind and the life we hoped to have again someday. Upon my brother's death, our father's gold watch came to me.

When my grandson, Mark, and his wife, Meredith, had my first great grandchild, Lyla, I marked the occasion of her birth by giving her my

father's gold pocket watch. Then, when Meredith was pregnant again, I announced that my Bar Mitzvah watch would go to my second great-grandchild. Lo and behold, she gave birth to twins – Hannah and Abby! What to do with the Bar Mitzvah watch now! I thought to myself, if I can't find an answer to it, no one can! I thought hard and long and decided to give it to Mark to keep in trust for his first grandchild. There has to be an answer for everything.

Mark and Meredith are great parents and their beautiful little girls are a great joy in my life. Mark is also the Executive Vice-President of Beaver Street Fisheries. He started learning the business as a boy and he's now doing an excellent job. When my biographer asked Mark to tell her about himself and his relationship with family, here is what he said:

Mark Frisch

I've always wanted to be in the family business. From the time I was 13-years old, I worked at Beaver Street Fisheries every summer. My brothers and I all worked there in the summers, and we worked in all the departments.

There was only one time when I had any thoughts of going into anything else and that was when I was in 10th grade at Bolles. I was playing basketball and baseball that year and decided I might go into sports journalism, but that didn't last long. The family business is in my blood.

I'm the middle son [born 11/20/1980] and am now the Executive Vice-President of Beaver Street Fisheries. My older brother, Adam [born 11/12/1977), went to law school before deciding to go into the business. Adam is now in Purchasing with the company, and our younger brother, Steven [born 5/8/1984], is in Sales and Exports.

Memories of my grandparents center around Sunday night

dinners together as a family. We would go to local restaurants like Famous Amos or Applebee's or Quincy's – never anyplace fancy. My grandparents didn't like to show off. The major topic of conversation whenever our family got together was the business, whether it was Sunday dinner or Thanksgiving.

Papa Harry loves to joke around. He would always tell people, "My wife and I have an agreement. She makes the small decisions and I make the big ones." Then he would pause for a moment and look over at her and say, "She decides what the big and small decisions are!"

Papa Harry expected his grandchildren to bring him our report cards so that he could keep track of our grades. We looked forward to it. He would give us 25 cents for an A, and God forbid we had a C. We would discuss ways to improve, and he would negotiate with us on what he might pay us for improved grades. It was exciting!

We attended Solomon Schechter Day School from Pre-K to 6th Grade (now Martin Gottlieb Day School). It was a good education. When I went to Bolles in 7th Grade, it was an easy transition. My daughters, Lyla, Hannah and Abby, attend The Discovery School at the beach. It is an excellent school, too.

Grandma Lilo was way ahead of her time regarding healthy eating habits. She never hesitated to tell us we were eating too fast or eating the wrong foods. She was a great cook – especially fresh fish and soups.

I remember going to their beach condo with my cousins and going fishing with Grandma Lilo. We would catch whiting and pompano right off the pier. She was handy and could do a lot. She always had Welch's Grape Soda at the beach condo and I used to play with a little transformer toy. There weren't many toys there, so I remember that one well. We would go swimming together in the indoor pool. Grandma Lilo had her own water aerobics routine that took about ten minutes.

I remember going with my grandparents to the big duck pond off of Hendricks Avenue in the Granada area to feed the ducks. I must have been young because the duck pond seemed as large as Lake Michigan back then.

As a college kid working at the business during the summer, I had the privilege of eating lunch daily with Papa Harry, Uncle Karl, and my Dad when he was in town. They discussed the problems of the day – always business – and I got a better education listening to them than I did at the University of Florida Business School. Excellence is expected in our family. All of these men have been great mentors to me.

When I look back at what my grandfather and great uncle had – the strength and perseverance to get through their hardships and succeed, I'm in awe. If I am ready to complain about something, I usually stop myself. I think of what they went through – what my grandfather did in spite of his life struggles - and that helps me keep things in perspective. I owe everything in my life to my grandfather. He's been amazing to me and my family – his influence on our behavior has been huge.

Uncle Fred was known by us as the Grumpy Old Man. We kidded him and weren't afraid of him at all.

If you ask me what accomplishment in business makes me proud, I have to say that I feel I've done a good job of taking a lot of the burden off of my grandfather's shoulders. I've done my best to carry on his legacy of community outreach. Little by little, I've gotten to know the people he knows and I'm proud of the Frisch name in this community. This business has grounded me.

As far as philanthropy, there are two societal ills that truly touch my heart … food insecurity and homelessness. I wish that everybody had a place to sleep and meals to eat. My wife, Meredith, has taught me a lot about philanthropy. Her parents *are also big philanthropists in the community.*

My wife, Meredith Chartrand Frisch, is from a Catholic family. She converted to Judaism, although I never asked her to do that. Her parents brought her here from Manchester, New Hampshire when she was in kindergarten, so she basically grew up in Jacksonville. We alternate Thanksgivings with her family and mine.

I'm into sports and fitness. I love to travel. I've been to nearly every major city in the United States, usually combining business and pleasure. I've been to China, Vietnam and Japan.

The summer of 10th grade, in 1996, I went on a trip to Poland and Israel for six weeks with a Jewish Youth Group. There were about fifty of us, including our leaders. We had morning, afternoon and evening prayer daily. When we were in Poland, we were praying in the middle of a park and there were people stopping and jeering at us, yelling not-so-nice things at this group of fifty Jewish youth. When we got to Israel, we felt like we had come home. It was so welcoming. I was fluent in Hebrew when in elementary school and lost some of it when I went to high school and focused more on Spanish. I later got a tutor because I didn't want to lose the Hebrew language.

I have a strong Jewish background, from a cultural

**Mark and Meredith Frisch –
Wedding Day**

perspective, but am not religious. Being alone on the beach and watching the ocean, sunrise, waves … those inspire me. Those are great spiritual moments.

One of the great things we do for the employees at Beaver Street is put on our annual picnic. With more than 400 employees now, it is a big deal. They all come and bring their families. My assistant, Chaz Martin, has been in charge of the picnic for a few years now and it takes a great deal of planning for the food and games and activities our employees have come to expect. This past year, we reserved Metropolitan Park for the day and all of us had a great time.

My family after a long, happy day at the 2017 BSF Picnic!

* * * * *

My grandson, Adam, is the oldest of Ben's three sons, born on November 12, 1977. Adam worked as a lawyer for several years before deciding to come into the family business. Today, he travels the world buying seafood for our company as Director of Procurement. Adam is married to Sierra, a beautiful, brilliant attorney who is one of my favorite people. Here is what Adam said when asked to talk about his life and his memories of Lilo and me:

Adam Frisch

I graduated from Law School at the University of Florida and spent five years in bankruptcy and corporate law before going into the family business in 2008.

I'm now in charge of the Purchasing Department which includes international buying and procurement. While we're sleeping, the company receives 70 to 100 emails every night from countries all over the world – mostly from Asia.

I learned a lot about negotiating from many people at BSF. It's all about the buy and getting the right price. We buy millions of pounds of shrimp and other seafood a year. We hope Sea Best is destined to be a nationally recognized brand. Everybody at Beaver Street is involved in sales. We are selling our story every day … entrenched in buying and selling daily. We must have a feel for the market – we must know it like the back of our hand.

I think I was born here at the office. I remember at about six years old, walking into the fish market. It was one big room – like an upside-down U of ice chests with an office in back. My grandmother was always moving when she was in there – never standing still. I began working here when I was 13 – working in the warehouse. There were many more items in our inventory then. I loaded trucks every day. I remember getting screamed at for riding the forklifts.

When we visited my grandparents at the beach, we would go surf-fishing with my grandma Lilo. At their house on San Jose, we would swim at the indoor pool and use the sauna. That was a treat – we didn't have a pool at our house. I went to Solomon

Schechter Day School up to 7th grade, 8th at DuPont, and then to Bolles for 9th through 12th.

Dad traveled a lot and Mom took us to our ball games, etc. I loved sports – played basketball, baseball and flag football. I love the Jaguars now.

Papa Harry (my grandfather) has been the ultimate inspiration and mentor to me. When times are tough, I always put things into perspective and think of him and what he did. He was always driving home the work ethic. He emphasized it when

Mark, Steven and me with Papa Harry

we went over our report cards with him. He talked about how we would be rewarded in life for hard work and how we should never let anybody outwork us.

I met my wife, Sierra, in law school. We were married in 2010. She's a prosecutor with the State Attorney's Office – runs a tight household and is one of the smartest women I know. We have a great life together.

As far as philanthropy, I'm actively involved with the JCA and River Garden Foundation. It's important to give back. Growing up, we knew we were privileged, but there were no big perks – we were taught to stay humble and we didn't live like rich kids.

We shopped at Marshalls and Walmart and ate out at places like Famous Amos. I remember it was a big deal the day I got my first pair of Nike Airs. We weren't spoiled.

I got into law school after I realized that it would help me argue both sides of every issue – and it has helped a great deal with my critical thinking because, unfortunately, people will take advantage of you in business if you let them. I've had to learn to know when to hold 'em and when to fold 'em. I've also learned that people are the same all over the world – they want to do business with people they like. A handshake is more important than a contract. You do business with friends.

I take two-week Asian trips at least once per year – traveling mostly to Vietnam, Thailand, India, Indonesia and China, but to many other countries as well. The logistics are crazy sometimes. I consider it a successful trip when the mission is accomplished, I've met with everyone I planned to meet with and made it home safely. Recently, I took 23 flights on one trip – I made a record of it:

Jax to Atlanta	Jakarta to Ho Chi Minh
Atlanta to Tokyo	Can Tho to Danang
Tokyo to Bangkok	Danang to Nha Trang
Bangkok to Surat Thani	Nha Trang to Ho Chi Minh
Surat Thani to Bangkok	Ho Chi Minh to Guangzhou
Bangkok to Chennai	Guangzhou to Qingdao
Chennai to Goa	Qingdao to Shanghai
Goa to Chennai	Shanghai to Macau
Chennai to Singapore	Hong Kong to Seattle
Singapore to Jakarta	Seattle to Atlanta
Jakarta to Surabaya	Atlanta to Jax
Surabaya to Jakarta	

I remember going to Israel with my grandparents when I was 13 and visiting with our relatives in Northern Israel. I

Harry, Sierra and Adam

saw where Dad and my Uncle Karl were born. There is an aura to Israel – it's almost a calming feeling to see an Israeli soldier with an M-16. I remember I felt almost an electric connection with the people and place – almost like you want to kiss the ground.

My grandfather is the ultimate inspiration to me and to so many others. Recently, I was with a Chinese supplier who has a picture of him and Papa Harry that was taken when he came to visit Beaver Street. He told me that Harry is his role model and that his goal is to work until he's 100, too.

My grandparents were a perfect match. They were constantly working to stay humble no matter how much they had and how hard they worked. At work, Papa Harry was and is the boss. I think his secret to longevity is staying active and staying humble – rather than getting cocky and arrogant, he and my grandmother always said they were in the right place at the right time and, with hard work, they were able to achieve success.

There's an inner joy about my grandfather. He's been called a good luck charm. A hug from him is supposed to bring luck – I think it's working for the Jaguars right now!

* * * * *

Steven is Ben's youngest son, born May 8, 1984. He is head of Export Sales for Beaver Street Fisheries and he, too, is a college graduate. All of my grandsons graduated from college and still say I'm their main role model, which is quite an accomplishment, since I only went to the 7th grade. Steven is musical. He loves music and talks about it a lot.

Steven Frisch

As my brother, Mark, mentioned a big memory of mine with our grandfather was sitting on his lap at the kitchen table going over the report cards. For an A you would get $1 and so on. However, I don't know what he did, but we would always end up with a couple hundred bucks!

Adam, Papa Harry, Governor Rick Scott, Mark and me.

I can go on for days and days, but everyone will tell you that my grandfather has so many sayings its crazy. The biggest one which is the title of this book is USE YOUR HEAD. But the saying in Hebrew is "Not with Strength, but with your head." And he always would tell us to sleep on every major decision over 2 nights. Don't act off your emotions.

Today, I work full-time at Beaver Street with my brothers

and my grandfather. It is a job that is in my blood. I remember the first time I actually ever made $1 from working and that was at my grandma's fish market. I believe it was a mullet that I sold, wrapped it up in some white paper, scotch-taped it and the customer gave me $1. I went and gave it to the store manager, who I believe who was Joni Moss and then she went to my grandma with it, but then my grandma said I could keep it. I thought I was the richest 5-year old on Earth!

Another memory about growing up was that my grandparents would always have 4th of July out at their beach house. The entire family would get there around lunch time, cook out all day and night and then light fireworks and watch them as well. This probably was a tradition for at least 15 years that I can remember.

Growing up, we either had to work during our breaks or go to camp. I always chose to work because I liked to make and save my money. And that's one thing that our grandfather always reminded us to do - save as much as possible because you never know one day you can wake up and it will be gone. And he said that because, as you know, that happened to him when the Nazi's came in.

I started working down in the warehouse at the age 13 and even when I graduated college, which was in 2006, I started back down in warehouse and had to work my way up to where I am today. There were no hand-outs with Harry. Papa Harry always wanted us to work in every department, so we knew everyone's job. He always wanted us to be better at their job than that person, so no one could really tell us what or how to do something because we would know it better than them.

In terms of my Dad, I never worked with him down in the Bahamas. As kids we would sometimes go down for vacation for a few days but other than that we weren't involved in that business. The one thing I can say I learned from my dad is that if you put your mind towards something, you can make anything happen and really be anything you want in life. He went down to the Bahamas with his uncle right after he graduated college, and he was doubted and told it wouldn't work out. Forty or so years later, he has created a powerhouse company in the islands.

Personally, I am not involved with one specific charity or foundation. However, one thing I do every year at the end of the year/holiday season is donate my entire wardrobe to a charity for the homeless/less fortunate. This is something I have been doing for about 4 years now.

I also have a passion for music. I love to sing. I got this talent from my grandma on my mom's side, and also from my mom. I remember hearing my mom sing when I was a kid and the first time I ever sang in front of a group I was probably 6 years old. I always wanted to be a music superstar or a professional athlete. I played football for two years at FSU, but the business was our real priority. However, my passion for music, which is a hobby of mine, turned into me discovering a hiphop artist a couple of years ago and then in turn getting him a major record deal from arguably the most iconic record label there is which is def jam recordings. So that was a very big accomplishment for me personally because to break into music is almost impossible. And that goes back to what I said about if you work hard enough you can make things happen.

Not too many memories about my great uncle Fred, as I was young when he passed away. One memory would be when my cousin handcuffed him to his office seat and we couldn't find the key to unlock it. That incident has turned into a family legend that we still laugh about at get-togethers.

* * * * *

Karl and his first wife, Michelle, gave Lilo and me two beautiful grandchildren, Daniel and Erin. Daniel earned his doctorate degree in psychology and he now works for the State of Wisconsin as a prison psychologist. He's called Dr. Frisch, which makes me so proud of him. He loves his patients and his dogs, and I don't hear from him often enough, but when I do get a phone call from him, he always says he is happy and that makes me happy, too!

Erin and Daniel (ages 6 and 8, respectively)

Daniel Frisch

My fondest memories of my grandparents is going over to their apartment and spending time with them. Grandma Lilo would pull out the Schnitzel from the freezer and put it inside pita bread. We'd just sit and talk, as far back as I can remember – way up until college, we'd talk about nothing specific … just about their lives and the lessons they learned. They were trying to impart wisdom to me. This usually happened on weekends when both of them were home. I always called her Grandma Lilo and him, Papa Harry.

Honestly, looking back now, it was a lot about them trying to tell me of the things that happened in their lives because of the Holocaust – them having to leave their homes – and that you can lose everything you have in an instant. They wanted me to appreciate what I had. Papa Harry always told me to learn as much as I could learn ... no one can ever take away what you have in your head.

I got my doctorate in psychology at Nova Southeastern University and what my Papa Harry taught me about learning may have been one of the biggest reasons I went into this field. There's so much to learn. People at work call me "Doc" but I don't go by that ordinarily.

Yes, I love animals. I have two German Shepherds, a Chocolate Lab and a miniature Pincher. And no, I didn't go into the family business.

One of the biggest lessons I learned from my grandfather and my father was that you have to do what makes you happy. If you enjoy what you do, you'll never work a day in your life. I've heard Papa Harry say that so many times.

I love what I do and I didn't love the idea of going into the family business. I worked there with my cousins over summer and spring breaks when I was growing up ... but it wasn't necessarily the fish business, it was the buying and selling – what they do is buy and sell and that's not what I was cut out for.

My grandfather, dad, uncle – business was discussed on all occasions – holidays and every day. It was always part of every family gathering – disagreements on how to run things – do certain things – different philosophies – there was always discussion about business, but there were fun parts of holiday gatherings, too, and good family memories.

I still think the biggest gift I ever received from my grandparents would be just to learn everything you can – be curious about things. Even now, when I watch TV, it's a science or history channel or a documentary about real life – as much time as I've spent with my grandfather, I would say there are so many facets about him I still don't know. He lives his life in the sense that he's super loyal to particular synagogues that helped him, even though he always says he's not a religious man. Any time they need anything, he's always there. He's done a lot for a lot of people – not just synagogues – the whole community.

On some kind of unconscious level, I'm giving back – using what they taught me when I was sitting around with them and listening to the talks we had. That's kind of what I do for work – I listen and talk – when you're doing therapy, you're listening and imparting wisdom – it's more structured, but it is what I do – and what they always did with me. I relate my childhood to what I'm doing now. I do it for personal reasons – learning how to talk to people and how they want to be treated.

The second biggest lesson I learned from my grandfather was how to treat people – whether it's a prisoner or the president – a bum on the street – it doesn't matter – people are people – they are human beings. That's one of the reasons Papa Harry was so successful – he always treated people like people. I would very much bet that if you talk to my coworkers or the inmates on my caseload, they would have positive things to say about the way I work. It's how you deliver things. If you talk to people like they are human beings and try to help find solutions - voice your frustrations and let them voice theirs – find out how we can solve this problem. That's what he's always done.

Specific details I remember about Grandma Lilo are going fishing with her. We'd come back to the condo afterwards and I'd spend more time with her than him there. The lessons I learned from her and from them – it helped me forge my path. He still loves his work and I love mine.

The pride and passion in the work shows through. She was always into mind and spirit thing – religious in the sense that there's a bond and brotherhood among the Jewish people and *that was something you could feel in her. I find organized religion, in general, hypocritical, but what I felt in my grandmother was real. She and Papa Harry were perfect for each other.*

Funny story about Uncle Fred … Erin and I went to the office with Dad on weekends sometimes. We'd play around and go through his desk drawers and walk around the office. Half the people still work there that did back then. One time, my sister found a pair of handcuffs in the office – she handcuffed Uncle Fred to a chair and we couldn't find the key. It took quite a while and it wasn't funny at the time, but looking back at it – it was hysterical. He wasn't a pleasant man under the best of circumstances.

One quote I always attribute to Papa Harry is "Don't let the door hit you where the sun doesn't shine on your way out."

Anything Papa Harry puts his mind to, he can do. Nothing is impossible if you decide you can do it. Like my grandfather decided what he was going to do and he did it. That's how he is. You work hard, and you can always figure things out.

School, life, maintaining my house up here – all of it is good. I moved from beach weather to snow – been here three years and I love it.

* * * * *

Our granddaughter, Erin, was a special gift – a girl! Her pretty little smiling face delighted her grandmother and me – and her girlish ways were just a little bit unfamiliar to us, with our big family of boys! She, like the boys, came into work at the business, but we didn't expect her to do the things the boys had to do. She was a girl! One thing she definitely picked up from her grandmother was her healthy habits – in fact, Erin ended up being a nurse at Wolfson Children's Hospital. She's a popular nurse and everyone over there loves her. I'm proud of her and what she's accomplished.

Erin Frisch

I wasn't around my grandparents a lot as a kid. I remember things like Grandma Lilo taking me fishing at the pier sometimes. When I was old enough to stand behind the counter - she let me push the buttons on the cash register. Grandma Lilo and Papa Harry had a pecan tree – Grandma Lilo and I used go to the picking tree and pick pecans. Her house was a very healthy place – we wanted candy and soda – but we didn't get it there. She was always ahead of time – she hated that I dried my hair and used chemicals to straighten my hair. She put beer and egg on my hair to condition it. She would be so happy today to know that I'm finally health-conscious. I don't even like medicine – I like homeopathic vitamins and supplements. Grandma Lilo always told me I was a Sagittarius, like her. My birthday is on December 20th – a week after hers – and being a Sagittarius makes me a people person – outgoing – getting along – seeking education – always wanting to learn. That was her and that is me.

Papa Harry was always so busy with business – both Pop and my Dad – they talked of nothing else. When holidays came it was always about work. Look at him now – he still works six

Erin and Daniel Frisch

days a week. I once told him he's the smartest man I know, and he said, "You must not know too many people." If you take the time to listen, he is so smart – he's brilliant. He could be the next president if he was younger. Everyone gets along with him. He knows everybody in the city. When I first started at Wolfson, I got to know the lunch guy. I'm friends with everyone – just like he is. I try to be like him. He's a role model to a lot of people. He's very smart and business oriented.

He has such a sense of humor. I remember that he had surgery on his neck and at the Christmas lunch at work, someone asked him about the big scar on his neck. "Oh, I just got back from Baghdad," he said. He is like a little kid. My Dad likes to pull pranks on people and tell jokes, too – probably got it from him.

Grandma Lilo let us have soy milk and almond milk only, but Pop loved his sweets. We'd find M&Ms sometimes, but she said it was for Papa Harry – she said he could have just a few at a time.

I graduated from FCCJ with my two-year degree in December

of 2010 – then graduated from JU in December of 2012. There is a lot of Grandma Lilo in me – always wanting to learn - chasing after education. Not with the strength of your muscles but with the strength of your brain, she would say. She always pushed education – don't stop learning, she'd say.

Being the only granddaughter feels special. I know Papa Harry loves me and would do anything for me. My Dad goes to see Papa Harry every Sunday and I always think I should go, too, and surprise him. My fiancé lost his step-mom and it was so sad. I lost my grandmother, but I've still got my Papa Harry.

Every memory I have of my grandparents is a positive memory. I loved Grandma Lilo and I love Papa Harry.

* * * * *

אויב צײַט איז געלט האָב איך קיין צײַט ניט.

Oyb tsayt iz gelt,
hob ikh keyn tsayt nit.

If time is money,
I don't have any time.

Oyb tsayt iz gelt, hob ikh keyn tsayt nit.

If time is money, I don't have any time.**

CHAPTER NINE: Times Change ... But I Stay the Same

Today, at age 95, I still go into the office five days a week. We used to work from 7 a.m. to 7 p.m., but now I arrive between 8:30 and 9:00 a.m. and stay until around 3 p.m. I climb the two flights of stairs with no assistance. Every minute of my time is spent as productively as possible.

I always joke that I will live to 120, but just in case my life is shorter, I will be as independent as I can for as long as I can.

**Illustration courtesy of Johanna Kovitz, www.yiddishwit.com*

Harry Frisch and Lathun Brigman – like brothers!

My assistant Tammy Pate, her assistant Laura Rhoden and Beaver Street's General Manager Lathun Brigman are all in the front office with me every day and they help me do what I do. I like being in the middle of all the action, and believe me, there is a lot of action in the front office of Beaver Street!

On my desk, I have a great photo of Lathun and me. He's been with Beaver Street Fisheries for thirty years and I depend on him completely. I trust him like a brother.

Nearly every day, Tammy and Lathun and I eat lunch together. Tammy, who has been with me for 22 years, keeps track of my schedule and tells me who I'm eating lunch with on any given day, and no matter who it is – Senator Bill Nelson, Sheriff Mike Williams, Congressman John Rutherford, UNF President John Delaney, Mayo's CEO Dr. Gianrico Farrugia – whoever has requested a lunch with me or been invited to join me – Tammy and Lathun are usually there, too.

Sometimes we go to lunch at the River Club, sometimes to other restaurants around

Harry and Norm Abraham at Two Doors Down

town, and sometimes we stay at Beaver Street Fisheries and go upstairs to the third floor and sit in my "Two Doors Down" booth.

We used to go to a restaurant called "Two Doors Down" so often that Tammy would call the owner, Norm Abraham, to let him know we weren't coming and he could let someone else sit in my reserved booth.

Sadly, Two Doors Down closed in November of 2015 and we still miss it. Everyone who was someone in the town of Jacksonville, and actually, in the State of Florida, used to come to Two Doors Down. It was a special meeting place where people could enjoy good, simple food and excellent conversation. When Two Doors Down closed, Norm Abraham gave me my special booth so that I could keep a piece of the place forever. I was so excited to hear that he is back in the restaurant business as the host at the new River & Post in Riverside. When I went in and saw him, I suggested we call it "Three Doors Down."

Chef McCool of FSCJ visiting with Harry at Café Frisch

Recently, Tammy and Lathun and I went to lunch at the new Café Frisch at Florida State College of Jacksonville's downtown campus. It is open for lunch and dinner on Tuesdays and Thursdays, and the cuisine is prepared by the Culinary Students at FSCJ. I'm proud to have had a big part in making this restaurant possible. When we go, we are treated like royalty! On that day, Chef McCool, one of the professors, came to our table and talked about the culinary program and how much it was helping the students to have a real restaurant where they can share what they are learning. Tammy and Lathun and I enjoyed our conversation with McCool, and our lunch was, of course, delicious!

Behind Lathun's desk at work is a funny photo of me looking like a gangster. It says, "THE REAL BOSS," but without Lathun by my side for all these years, I could not have been as good a boss as I've been. We have a deep love and respect for each other.

One day, while sitting at his desk, Lathun reminisced about his memories of Beaver Street in days gone by and right up until now.

Lathun Brigman hard at work at his desk at Beaver Street Fisheries

Lathun Brigman

After thirty years with this company, I feel like I know Harry's answer to a question even before he speaks. Our mindsets are very much the same and he seldom surprises me, but sometimes he'll come up with something and I'll think, how did he come up with that? Harry is an unusual man. For instance, he is Jewish and I'm

Christian, but our spiritual differences have never been an issue. In fact, Harry and my former pastor, Mac Brunson, at First Baptist Church of Jacksonville, are friends and sometimes Harry asked him to have lunch with him so they could have a theological discussion. Harry's intelligence and interest in other people is as strong as ever.

I grew into this job. When I first came to Beaver Street, Harry had me working in operations, accounting and even in the warehouse. He wanted me familiar with different parts of the business and that's a good thing that he does with nearly everyone he hires.

Like everyone who knew her, I miss Lilo Frisch. She was a wonderful lady. Back in years past, if there was a tough account to collect, Ms. Lilo would collect the money. She went after them and wouldn't take no for an answer. My wife, Debbie, and I have been close to Harry and Lilo. We went out together often for social events and most of our conversations centered around work. You talk about work even when you're not there. Lilo was a strong family woman – a strong force for good. She did what she could to help people recover from illnesses. If she saw a person that needed some soup or something, she would make sure that person got soup. She always wanted to help.

Fred Frisch was probably a genius. He was one of the smartest men I've ever met. He spoke about nine different languages and was a tireless worker. His hobby was work. He was brilliant. Over the years, I worked very closely with both Fred and Harry. The brothers made decisions together. They didn't make a decision unless they were in complete agreement. They were always open for my opinion, but there were very few times when I would have done anything differently. I'm fine with what they've done with this company. They based their business on the Ten Commandments. I'm fine with that.

* * * * *

Wednesday, January 24, 2018 was a fairly typical day at the office for me. I got there around 8:30 a.m. and my personal accountant, Jeff Mickler, brought some documents to me. Together, we went over the accounts. Jeff handles all of my personal business and my private corporation, HF Investments, as well as doing the accounting for the Frisch Family Foundation. He is one of my most valuable assets and I am thankful to have him by my side.

Jeff Mickler & Harry – Working together on January 24, 2018

Laura Rhoden came to Beaver Street in 2016 to work directly with me and assist Tammy. On January 24, 2018, Laura sat at my desk as she usually does and helped me review my mail, as well as purchase orders and wire-transfers. Then we went through the checks waiting to be signed. As she sat by my side and presented each check, I signed some of them and indicated to her which ones I wanted her to set aside because I had a question about the charge or the invoice. Laura has worked with me long enough to know exactly what I need. She is wonderful, very helpful and detail-oriented. She told my visitor that she is so impressed with my common sense – that I have such good ideas that she goes home every day and shares them with her husband, Ed, and they have started doing the same things at home! Once a check has been signed, it either goes in the regular pile of checks

Laura Rhoden & Harry on January 24, 2018 – typical day at the office

or to a special slot designated for certain people and departments. Then Laura and I go over the checks I had a question about. On the 24th of January, I had a question about an electricity invoice and a young woman from that department came and answered my question to my satisfaction and I signed the check. Laura explained to my visitor that employees at Beaver Street are very much aware that I am watching everything, and they like coming in to talk with me about why a certain charge was made for something. It makes them feel good to know I am still interested in the operations of Beaver Street.

"He remembers everything!" Laura declared to my visitor, grinning at me. "He keeps me on my toes!" She explained that everything in the office has a place every single time and that such organization leads to creative ideas that work.

On January 24th, I received a delightful email addressed to "Hansi" (that's me) from Alex Frisch of Wein, Austria, the son of my first cousin,

Gerhardt Frisch. Alex was happy to announce the birth on December 20, 2017 of his son, David Maximillian Frisch! I sent him back an email of congratulations! I still keep in touch with many of my relatives and Lilo's relatives around the world.

Tammy and Harry on Ocean 14 walkway

Following a busy start of the day, Tammy took me to a late morning appointment and our visitor rode with us. We then drove over to visit my condo on the 7th Floor at Ocean 14.

It was a chilly, blustery day and we wore our coats as we walked on the outside walkway to the condo. I usually enjoy sitting out on the balcony overlooking the ocean but not that day! It was too windy! Tammy noticed that a closet door was needing repair and she was determined to repair it rather than have me call the maintenance people. It was a challenge, but as always, Tammy rose to the challenge and got the door fixed. I can always depend on her to do more than is expected. She is truly my right-hand person and I couldn't do without her.

Tammy is one of several people at Beaver Street who are second or even third-generation employees. Tammy's mother, Mavis Van Landingham (later Voss), was employed here back in the 1980's as an assistant in National Sales.

Today, three of Mavis's daughters are now employed at this family-oriented company. Tammy's sister, Paige Savitz, began working at Beaver Street Fisheries (BSF) back in 1982 and is now Director of Imports. Tammy began her employment in 1996 and her sister, Delane Johns, started in 2007, and is Customer Service Manager.

As with many BSF employees, it is truly a family affair with Tammy. When her sister, Delane Johns, needed a job in 2009, Tammy recommended that I interview her. She qualified in every way for the job except for one thing ... Delane was a smoker and I was determined to make Beaver Street a smoke-free workplace. I told her I would hire her if she stopped smoking. She said she would take the job and promised to quit smoking. When she asked me how long she had to do that, I told her, "You have from now to the door." She quit smoking that day and tells me she has never regretted it. Today, Delane heads up our Customer Service Department and cares very much about our customers and their satisfaction with our product.

**BSF Sisters –
Delane, Tammy and Paige**

When asked to share her thoughts about me for this book, Tammy Pate said she was overwhelmed with many thoughts and memories of interactions between us. She wrote that she has learned many life lessons from me, most of which are simple common sense. She says some of those lessons are as follows:

Tammy Pate

· *I am open to discuss anything ... you never know what you don't know*
· *Just be nice to people*
· *Your reaction to someone is the only power they have over you*

Most of the other lessons are included in his Good Business Practices, but I see him live these things out in his daily life. He doesn't just say them, he lives them. The most evident thing about Harry Frisch is what a generous person he is. He is the least selfish person I've ever met. He looks out for Harry, too, but he would give you the shirt off his back if you needed it, or the last dollar (or $2 bill) in his wallet. He has known what it means to be without and not know where his next meal is coming from and he knows what it is to have in abundance. Because he has had to work so hard for everything he has, he detests laziness and/or the attitude of 'gimme gimme gimme.' You work for what you want in life. That's what he did.

There has been nearly no limit to our conversations at times, from medical to spiritual. We have discussed at length things spiritual in nature and I long for him to see and accept the Gift that has been given, but this is where we agree to disagree. Even so, since we have lunch together with others nearly every day, out of his own thankfulness and his respect for me, there is always a pause for prayer at a meal, to thank God for all of our blessings at the table and in the business. So many of his "good practices" can actually be found in scripture as Biblical principles to live by.

Another very evident observation is his love for his family and for Israel. He has fond memories of his birthplace in Vienna, Austria. I remember stories of his entire family living in that huge house of three levels; parents, grandparents and uncles with their families. So many family members were lost in the Holocaust. He cries when he talks about it. His and his brother's escape to their haven of safety is probably what drives his love for Israel. Although the trip there was horrendous, they made it! He met his wife there and has many fond memories of Independence Day, driving the jeep in the parade with his uniform on. He was so proud to be a part of that. They had to fight for that too, which made it all the more precious.

To describe my relationship with Mr. Frisch, I will use his words to do it. He always says we have a "father/daughter, mother/son" relationship. He truly has been like a father to me. From simple life instruction, life example, what to do, what not to do, how to speak to people, how to love people and give where there's a need (and how to NOT GET TAKEN). Simply put, I love him. He's precious and infuriating at times, but that's what having a father/son is – you love them, help them, care for them, look out for them – you love them. And I love him dearly.

Tammy and Harry at BSF

* * * * *

In addition to Lathun and Tammy, who are my right and left-hands, along with the daily help of Jeff Mickler and Laura Rhoden, there are so many other people at Beaver Street Fisheries that I count on. There is no way to pay tribute to all of them in one book, but there are some that must be noted and quoted.

For instance, Jeff Edwards, our Chief Financial Officer, was the one who finally got me to hire my biographer, Susan D. Brandenburg, to help me write this book. Susan had written the World War II Memoir of Jeff's Dad, Marvin Edwards, Now It Can Be Told – Tales of the OSS, and Jeff insisted that I get on with writing my story. For that, I'm grateful to Jeff, and for so much more. Jeff has been with me since 1983 … thirty-five years … and has helped make Beaver Street Fisheries what it is today. He came to me from a great big corporation, Charter Company, that had fancy offices all over the country and in a big high-rise office building downtown. Jeff was asked to remember when I hired him, and what happened next:

Jeff Edwards

Beaver Street Fisheries was located in a simple warehouse that was a real contrast to the Charter Company offices, but my parents taught me not to ever judge a book by its cover. It was as humble inside as it was outside. The ceilings were so low, you almost felt like you needed to duck down, and the offices were small cubicles, including Harry Frisch's office. It was not at all what I was accustomed to, but after interviewing with Harry Frisch, I knew I was in the right place. Harry asked me what I wanted. I told him, and he hired me. It was that simple. I spent the next six months cross-training with the company – learning about everything from the warehouse to purchasing to packing. There were no titles at the time, although I am now called the CFO and have been doing that job for more than three decades.

When I first began with the company, Harry was always there and his brother, Fred, was traveling nearly all the time. Both brothers were streetwise and smart like foxes – Harry taking care of the home-front and Fred doing the wheeling/dealing on the outside. Fred Frisch was a restless soul – he needed to get on an airplane and go to Latin America, South America, the Caribbean, the Orient – wherever – he needed to be out there negotiating.

As businessmen, the Frisch brothers played serious games and if they lost, they didn't lose twice. They had hearts of gold, but you didn't want to cross either of them. Fred was known as eccentric. He was the king of the back-handed insult. Traveling with Fred was an adventure. He would walk up to strangers and spin yarns, taking a ridiculous story path, and people would believe him.

Fred had a gruff way about him. We would be laughing one moment and the next, he'd be yelling, "Edwards, get in here! I need to see you now!" I got to know both Harry and Fred so well that I almost always knew the answer before they asked the question. Fred spoke several foreign languages fluently and would sometimes pretend that he only spoke English so that he could eavesdrop on the conversations going on around him in a foreign country. He was clever and had a tough exterior, but like Harry, he felt there were no boundaries to finding a solution for whatever problem presented itself.

I had been with Beaver Street for only ten weeks when Mary and I got married. Fred and his wife, Bessie, came to our wedding. We were blown away. Bessie died of breast cancer. She was the one love of Fred's life and he stayed by her bedside at M.D. Anderson when she passed away. Later, I mentioned to Fred that I had an aunt in Maryland with a rare type of cancer and we thought we might try to get her in at M.D. Anderson. He *instantly responded, "Do you want me to make the call now?" I was touched by his generosity. She ended up going to the National Institute of Health, but I've never forgotten how quickly he responded with an offer of help.*

Jeff Edwards, Lilo, Harry, Tammy Pate and Thora Rose

Harry and Fred both thought of out-of-the-box solutions and would eventually find a way to solve the problem where everybody involved could save face. It was important to them that people retain their dignity. As a result, they avoided nasty confrontations on legal issues by working hard to accommodate the customer. Harry was and is an expert at this. I never met anyone who didn't like Harry. When there is a problem, it gets solved. In the whole world, there is no one I know who respects people more and receives more respect than Harry Frisch.

When we sold the food division to Sysco, there were customers who were actually crying. They were emotionally connected to us – knowing we had given up more than we needed to in order to accommodate them and nobody else would do what we did. We treated our customers like family – still do.

For a company our size, we do more for the community than many companies much larger – we do so many things that people don't even know about. The philanthropic role of our company is something I truly value and I've represented Beaver Street

Fisheries (as well as myself personally) on many boards in this town over the years.

Lilo and Harry were a great couple – always caring and sharing with others. My wife, Mary, and I went to many charity events with them. Lilo was a strong woman with definite opinions. She always dressed impeccably and loved fine art. Whatever fine art is in their home, she brought it there. Harry always said that he was the head of the family and she was the neck that told him which way to turn. After Harry's mother died, Lilo took over the retail fish store at Woodstock and Serenac on Beaver Street. She was a business woman who knew what she was doing and truly cared for the employees – treated them like family. In fact, as I said, the family aspect rules at Beaver Street.

Harry and Fred were like the glue that held the company together – they complimented each other. Harry was the face of the company and Fred pursued business on the outside. There were definitely two heads, and they discussed every business concern and addressed the ever-changing challenges with flexibility. There was never an org chart at Beaver Street. We are family. Our customers love us – they know we'll always give it our best shot to meet and exceed their needs.

Harry can charm anybody and has done so for over 60 years. Nobody at Beaver Street puts on airs – it is the antithesis of a typical corporate atmosphere. This is your family here and people know it. Histrionics are compartmentalized and handled quietly. The business is conservatively managed. Harry makes things happen – in fact, he is always looking for problems to solve because that is what ultimately makes him happy. Harry is a great role model. I've learned so much from him, especially about common sense.

* * * * *

When Jeff Edwards talked about Fred and me finding solutions for every problem, he was pretty accurate, but I have to say that having a lawyer on our staff has helped a great deal, too. Mike Gvozdich came to work for us twenty-five years ago, in 1993. He had moved here from Washington, D.C. and his sister-in-law, Linda Williams, was working for us. He was our company lawyer from the beginning, although we did have him train with sales and in the warehouse for a little bit, so he would be familiar with all the workings of the company. Mike has become such an important part of Beaver Street Fisheries. I depend on him and think of him as family.

Asked why he chose to work for Beaver Street Fisheries as the staff attorney, here is Mike's reply:

Mike Gvozdich

The one thing I hate is to be bored. This place is not boring. I never know what is going to confront me from one day to the other. It's interesting and sophisticated. It's an international company and I was impressed with the company and the Frisch family from the beginning. The reason I'm still here is that I love the Frisch's and I love Jacksonville. I love the way we do business. It's constantly changing and we're always looking for new ways to do things. It's never mundane. The more I stayed here, the more interested I got. I'm both a lawyer and a CPA and had practiced in both areas when I came to Jacksonville. When I first started here, I handled most of the tax stuff, but now I'm more of a big picture person. We are the legal department – my assistant and me – and we handle what litigation there is, which is almost non-existent. For a company our size, we have virtually no litigation, but there is always something going on – product liability lawsuits and slip and falls that don't amount to a lot of money. Harry has created a company culture that stays away from litigation if at all possible. Harry's position is that we don't make any money when we're sitting in the courtroom, so we avoid getting sued or suing whenever we can.

Over the years, I've developed a personal relationship with Harry. Harry and Fred ran the company when I started, and the dynamics were different then. They each had their own way of managing, but they made joint decisions and I learned to deal with them both. Harry has extremely strong principles and he goes by those principles, no matter what. He's always been like that.

Fred always called me a 'so-called lawyer,' saying I learned nothing in school and that his education was ten times better than what I got in college and law school. Neither of the brothers ever put any credence in college or higher learning – they believed you get your education in the school of hard knocks.

I always feel that Fred is looking down and watching over us. I learned so much form both of them about business. How to run a business and how to interact with people, business-wise. Harry has been a great mentor to me. He is a great man and I don't know how many hundreds of people have benefitted from knowing him.

Jacksonville has become my home town now. I grew up in Ohio but then moved to Washington, D.C., and my roots were not that well-settled until I got here. This is a nice place to live and I've become an East Coast person. Harry is responsible for a lot of the way I feel about Jacksonville. He loves this city. When I first got here, it smelled like the papermills, but it's grown a great deal on many levels and it's beginning to realize its potential. My position has evolved and I've become more involved in community stuff, although not as much as Jeff and Lathun.

Harry has had a positive affect on my life. He's gotten me to look at things differently in all facets of life – community service, for instance. You need to give back to the community and I *spend a lot of hours going to events on behalf of Beaver Street. I see how vibrant Harry is at 95, and he's made me less sensitive about retirement. He has accomplished so much. He comes in and talks to me about different things – history and how his family went through the holocaust and came to the U.S. with nothing and started a little fish company. I said to him, 'Harry, I bet you never thought that it would grow into what it is today.' He responded, 'Yeah, I knew it would be big.' He had a vision and he dreamed it would be this successful.*

Mike Gvozdich, Harry, and Lathun Brigman - 2018

Both Harry and Fred were hard on the outside and soft on the inside. I remember that whenever Fred talked about his late wife, Bessie, he would tear up, and now Harry's the same way about Lilo. It's impressive to me that he's still that emotional about her. He and Lilo never argued and he says there was never a four-letter word spoken in their house. I've sat there and listened to his emotional words – he means what he says and says what he means. He's never duplicitous. Harry is the real deal.

* * * * *

Darrell Glover was 16 when he was hired on at Beaver Street on December 16, 1966 (52 years ago!) to work in the retail market for my mother. As so often happens, Darrell's mother was already working as a bookkeeper for us when he came to work here. He can talk about the early days because he remembers them like it was yesterday. Darrell recently tried to retire, but I talked him into partial retirement (as I say in my Points of Good Business, Keep the Old People ... Darrell Glover knows more about our business than any two people who are working there today).

Darrell Glover

It was the first day of Christmas vacation and I came in after school that day. I needed the job because I was playing sports at Paxon High school and that cost money my family didn't have. There were two managers in the retail market – Big John and Little John. That first day, Big John handed me a broom and told me to sweep out the floor in front of the counter space. Little John then handed me a mop and told me to mop the floor in front of the counter space. Then it was time to take the fish off the showcase that we didn't sell and put it in iced fish boxes and then put them in the cooler. We had to turn them so that the fish on the bottom were now on the top. I learned so much that day - went home dead tired but feeling good about working. I made 90 cents an hour, working for two weeks during Christmas break. Baseball didn't start until March, so I kept on working after school.

I remember my first paycheck. I got $1 an hour instead of 90 cents and thought I'd gotten a raise, but then I found out that minimum wage had gone from 90 cents to a dollar. I worked with Mrs. Rappaport, Harry's mother. She would sit in the little window of the market and watch us. I always felt like her eyes were on me. I was the youngest one there and she watched every move I made, or it seemed like it. She was a short woman who drove a Cadillac and she smoked a lot. I was afraid of her. She was very tenacious. She didn't have to yell, she would just look at you and you knew not to do something wrong.

It was never easy growing up in this business – there are so many headaches. You have to ask questions, or you won't learn. I was 17 and working in the retail market when Queen Robinson showed me how to cut a fish. I had cut one with a grouper knife and was feeling proud of myself when she slapped me on my butt with the side of that knife. "That's not how you treat your customer!" she yelled. I had left too much meat on the bone. My thoughts had been to leave meat on there because Queen would dust and fry the backbones for lunch, but the customer always came first. I learned that the hard way. The retail market was always busy. Friday night we would close at 8 p.m. and until closing, there was just standing room – people lined up. Saturday was the same way.

After Mrs. Rappaport left, Miss Lilo was the woman sitting in the window, but she was different. She was such a caring person. I got sick back in the 1970's – had a bad flu and couldn't get out of bed. She kept checking on my welfare. She even brought by some soup for me. She was just a good person – if she saw you eating the wrong thing, she'd tell you. She was a very healthy person – way ahead of her time in knowing what to eat and what not to eat.

I felt like I would do better in the seafood business if I applied myself, so I chose to go into the seafood business at a time when all my friends were going to college. I stayed with this little company named Beaver Street Fisheries and today, I'm on every team and have enjoyed a great relationship with the company for more than 50 years. I'm dyslexic and Harry always worked with me on that. His understanding has meant a great deal to me, but in spite of being treated so well, I did leave one time, back in 1991. I had worked there my whole life, but I had a disagreement with another man who worked there, and I resigned.

I was gone for a year. The first month, Harry never said a word, but the second month, he called me to make sure everything was okay. I grew during that year, partnering with a guy named Davy Lamb and starting a company in the Southeast. Through that experience, I realized how much education I'd gotten through Beaver Street, and I went back stronger than ever.

I believe in right and wrong and I have no problems with who it is that is right or wrong. If somebody is wrong, I tell them they're wrong. I try to find a way to negotiate, and it gets better. I always had this thing with Harry – when he made what I considered a wrong judgment, I'd call him on it. Those things I do leave scars, I know, but right is right and I have to say what I believe is right. Harry is like my father. I spent more time with him than I did my own family. Any time it came up that I needed help, he was there for me.

I've enjoyed working in Bermuda for many years. Most of the time I'm out visiting the resorts, chefs, managers, buyers – I always make a point of taking somebody with me, so they can learn the laws of the island and so that the company won't suffer if something happens to me. That habit was instilled in me by Harry Frisch. I don't work for myself – I work for the company.

I've worked for the family from the very beginning.

Recently, I began doing something Harry used to do, but he can't do it at age 95. I walk the dry warehouse every day. I go down to the plant and look at the crabmeat, check things out. The people know I'm coming and they're used to seeing me there. I'm Harry's pair of eyes in the warehouse. Lathun goes down sometimes, too, and walks around on Harry's behalf.

Ben Frisch, Harry's son, and I came into the business at the same time. Ben is in the Bahamas and he is still an owner, in fact, he's picking up speed. He doesn't slow down at all. Now his sons are at the helm of the company. I think Beaver Street Fisheries will change because younger minds are different than older minds.

Harry and Fred were raised to understand the value of a dollar. There was a time in my life when I bought my second home. My home was bigger than Harry's home. His was a nice house, but not a big house. I learned so much from him and from his brother, Fred. Fred was the one who took me and educated me on how to buy a car. You don't negotiate a trade-in and buy a car. Those are two separate deals. You negotiate the new car first – make an offer and walk away. Then, when you've got the rock bottom offer, you ask about your trade-in. To this day, I've not been turned down one time.

Harry and Fred were great teachers. I've always learned as much as I could and tried to educate as many people as I could, so they'll never be able to say they don't know how to do something.

Harry is the greatest man I've ever met. Harry and Fred were equals, each in his own way. Harry is amazing. The thing that people don't know - you see him now and he seems so sweet – you didn't see him 40 years ago! He would yell and scream and be upset, then look at me and wink. He always did it when our profits were going through the roof – that's when he was the worst – it was crazy. He knew that when you go up you're going to come down. It didn't take me long to figure it out.

I've had good people around me, and the smartest people I know were the least educated people. I always tell Harry I probably should have quit school in the 6th grade since he quit in the 7th. Instead, I got a PHD – Paxon High Diploma.

If the good lord came down to me and said, "Glover, I'll make you the richest man in the world," I couldn't be richer. Raising my daughters was the highlight of my life – and the lessons I learned from Harry and Fred made me a better father and husband. They were the men who helped me put things into perspective for life.

Darrell and Harry

Beaver Street has been my life. If I had to do it over again, I wouldn't make any changes. I'd probably make the same mistakes over again. The one mistake I didn't make was recognizing that Beaver Street is the place that I belong.

* * * * *

Marshall Whitley remembers how it was back in the 1970's because I hired him when he was still in his teens back in 1975. Today, he's in National Sales, but back then he worked with Lilo in the retail fish market.

Marshall Whitley

My Dad was a shipping supervisor at the retail market and brought me to work one day when I was about ten years old, so I always knew about Beaver Street Fisheries and Harry Frisch as I was growing up.

After I graduated from Englewood High School in 1974, I went to work for a guy named Coleman, who owned Discount Seafood. I was about 18 or 19 years old and had married young, but it was a good job – I had a new pickup truck to drive, got a great Christmas bonus and I was happy.

My wife and I were at the Pic n' Save Buffet soon after Christmas and we ran into Harry and Lilo Frisch. He was a big important man and I was intimidated, especially when he came up to me and said, 'I need to talk to you. I want you to come work for me and run the retail market.' I told him I wasn't interested. I had a good job and I was satisfied. Harry wouldn't take no for an answer. He said, 'You really need to talk to me.'

The next day, my boss called me in to his office. He said, 'I got a call from Harry Frisch last night.' I assured my boss that I had turned Harry down when he offered me a job. My boss said, 'Harry Frisch can offer you more than I can. There's a huge future there and I promised him I'd have you talk to him.' He saw the big picture of Harry Frisch.

When I went in to talk to Harry, I told him I liked my job with Coleman. I had a new truck and a good bonus. I was happy. He wanted to know what kind of truck and what color it was. It was a blue Chevy. He wanted to know how much my bonus was.

Marshall Whitley
National Sales (43 years)

He pulled a piece of scrap paper out of the garbage can and wrote something on it and slid it across the desk. 'What do you think?' he asked. The figure he had written was much more than my bonus. He asked, 'How much are you making?' Again, he wrote something on a piece of scrap paper and slid it across the desk. It was much more than I was making. I still had the nerve to ask about the new pickup truck. He told me not to worry about it – just report for work the next day. When I came in the next day, he handed me a set of keys for an identical blue Chevy truck.

He hired me to work for Lilo. I was very nervous. I'd never worked for a female before, but what an amazing woman she was! She brought me a piece of fruit every day and said 'Eat this. It's good for you!' Her yearly reviews of me were detailed and so appreciative. On her sons' birthdays, she would always buy me a shirt. Lilo loved to fish. She'd sell the fish she caught at the market – those that she didn't take home to cook.

I was a fresh pair of eyes in the market and I had some ideas. I talked to Harry about upgrading the building with stand-up freezers rather than the casket, reach-in freezers they had. It turned out to be a wonderful idea. You could see the fish through the glass! Lilo started selling 5-pound boxes of shrimp at a discount and increased the sales tremendously. She would put ads in the entertainment section of the paper – Beaver Street Fisheries – Sale - 5 lb. box of Shrimp – and she'd always have a rope around the ad to make it stand out.

I was the retail manager there at the store. I'd open at 7 a.m. and she'd come in most afternoons. We had some interesting customers, to say the least. There was one lady who had a 50-pound cat that only ate jumbo lump crab meat. She came in every week and Lilo would help her. Lilo was a real people person – she loved to help everybody. My ex-wife went to FSCJ Cosmetology School and Lilo went there on purpose to get her hair done. She could have gone anywhere – she just enjoyed helping people. Harry and Lilo taught me about loving family.

Harry also taught me to be a center of the plate seafood specialist and to keep customers happy – no matter what. Lindsey at the Cloister – Sea Island Plantation – was the head buyer and Harry always told me to take good care of Lindsey and make sure she was happy. Harry had Tuesday morning meetings that started at 7 a.m. sharp – if you were five minutes early, you were late. One Tuesday, I was running 15 minutes early and Lindsey called. She had a problem. I spent a long time on the phone with her, watching the clock and sweating bullets.

I got to the meeting ten minutes late and Harry looked up at me and said, "Next time you're late, don't let the door hit you where the sun doesn't shine on the way out." Everybody was snickering as I sat down. After the meeting, I stopped Harry and told him that I was late because I was taking care of Lindsey. He smiled and said, "Oh, don't worry. I just did that for effect." I told him it was very effective!

Harry's attention to detail is almost uncanny. He's shrewd and so attentive in a quiet, unassuming way that he can really make you feel good about yourself. Forget Trump ... Harry's the best businessman I've ever seen. He's the true originator of the Art of the Deal!

* * * * *

Sam Kalil has been my good friend for longer than he's been my employee. I knew when I hired him that I could trust him to always do the right thing ... never lie, cheat or steal ... and to work hard to increase our territory. He sure has done that!

Sam Kalil

My sales territory is limited. It goes from the Atlantic Ocean to the Pacific Ocean. Walmart is my biggest customer. There are twenty-two different buyers – retail accounts and wholesale distributors – it's massive.

I've been here 34 years, and 11 years ago, my son, Scott, came on board. He's got a law degree and he's smart. We work well together. A few years ago, Walmart had a problem with the packaging of our lobster tails and there had been some theft, so Scott and I decided to do something about designing some new packaging. We were in Home Depot and saw a package that inspired us, so we redesigned our packaging in a similar style and got a patent on our design. For a while, only Walmart could use the package, but now other customers like Kroger and Albertsons are asking for it.

We're all over the country. Every day, we send out 30 to 40 truckloads of product – about 15 tons a week. Years ago, I had just left a financial services job and Harry called and said, "Come talk to me. I want to expand this business. Come talk to me."

Sam & Scott Kalil

Beaver Street was not like it is today. It was a hole in the wall. Harry and I sat on a couple of milk crates. He first wanted me to target a chain in Alabama called Bruno's and it took me three trips and numerous phone calls to do it, but we got Bruno's (since closed). I've since then put about 2 million miles on Delta Airlines. I try to sell to the Southeast and the Midwest rather than New York – because invariably when you sell to New York – there is a complaint. Harry will agree with me on that.

Harry and I were good friends before I started working for him. He gave me the tools and said, "You run this department." Now retail sales are about 60% of the business.

Harry will give you the shirt off his back – literally – he's that kind and generous, but he was a pistol back when I first came. He's never yelled at me, though, in fact, he still comes in my office and asks me "What's going on?" He knows I'll tell him.

One time I told him about this guy in the warehouse that was giving me a hard time. He called him into the conference room and started yelling at him, pounding the table, getting red in the face. I was afraid he was going to have a heart attack! You could hear him all over the building. He was screaming at the guy, "When Sam tells you to do something, it's just like I *told you ... do you understand? Do you understand?" The guy left the conference room, scared to death, and ran back to the warehouse. Harry came to the door, all calm and cool, and said, "How'd that go?"*

Harry's mind never stops working. He still marks every piece of mail that comes through here with a red crayon. He and Fred were great partners – Fred a world traveler and salesman on the outside – Harry in control here – the inside man.

* * * * *

Chris Wiles is in charge of all the maintenance here at Beaver Street and he does an excellent job. I feel like he's grown up here. He and his Dad, Bubba, and their whole family have been part of our family for many years.

Chris Wiles

My Dad, Lawrence "Bubba" Wiles, worked here for a few years before I did. I was hired by Kenny Higginbotham in 198l and went to trade school to learn how to work with the refrigeration system. That was 37 years ago and today, I'm the Maintenance Director for Beaver Street Fisheries with nine men supporting me in that situation – Two forklift mechanics, three production mechanics and four refrigeration mechanics.

We're a three generation Beaver Street Fisheries family – my daughter, Brooke Ashley Forhan, now works for Sam and Scott Kalil in sales on the Walmart account. She started eight to ten years ago and worked her way up from imports to sales. Advancement is good here, but it just means more to do.

I'd do anything for the Frisch family. They have seen me through two bouts of cancer and I never missed a paycheck. I've raised my three kids while I worked here, and for the past thirteen years, I was a single parent. Children have needs and this company is family-oriented and gives family support. That sort of kindness and consideration grows obligation. I'm definitely obligated to this company. I'm available any time night or day – I used to have a beeper on me at all times – now it's my phone, and I'm definitely on call.

I'm thinking ahead all the time about how we can get better. Harry instilled that in me. He was very strong about that, and when he could get around better, he'd be checking out every single inch of this place. He is still very much aware of what's going on.

**Chris Wiles –
Used to have a beeper –
now has cell phone!**

I now have three grandkids. I remember the company picnics so well – my kids loved them – the picnics started at Jeff Edwards' home at County Dock Road, and now they are so big we reserve Metropolitan Park. This company is the best!

* * * * *

Johnny Townsend came to work here when he was just a big lanky boy, and he says that "Miss Lilo" taught him how to be a business man. He is a valued employee today – in charge of Quality Control, which is one of the most important things we do … control all the quality of our products coming in and going out of Beaver Street.

Johnny Townsend

I was 18 years old and working for another company when my brother-in-law, Joe Lane, Sr., introduced me to Beaver Street Fisheries. I started working for Mrs. Frisch on January 28, 1983. I'd been going to FCCJ downtown campus, wanting to be in the data-entry field, so I worked part-time for Mrs. Frisch in her retail seafood store. I went on full-time soon and worked for Mrs. Frisch for eight years. I became the retail manager, working for her until May 14, 1994. Numbers are my thing – math has always been my strong suit. I can run numbers and dates off like hotcakes – no problem.

Mrs. Frisch taught me how to conduct myself in business. She taught me to be hardworking, determined and honest. She taught me the ins and outs of successful business. She was old-school – instead of shorthand, she gave me long-hand, and it was good. She wasn't easy, though. One day she'd come in sweet and other days she was hard to deal with. There were more sunshiny days than rainy ones, though. I learned to keep the people around me on point – be alert to my surroundings. Mrs. Frisch was very kind and

Johnny Townsend

generous but sometimes she had her moments. She could ride you from one end of the wall to the other, and the next day, shower you with cookies and be so nice.

I've grown up at BSF. Hard work and determination pay off.

I've learned that if you stay dedicated and focused and true to what you do, it's good steady employment. I've worked in many departments. Hard word plays a major role – being honest and doing the right thing.

I'm in charge of Quality Control (QC) and I inspect any seafood item that comes into Beaver Street, no matter where it comes from. We do everything the U.S. Department of Commerce does, but we do it first.

* * * * *

Art Pollan and I go back a long way – much longer than the thirty-plus years he's been working here at Beaver Street. Our families have been friends forever, as we had much in common with Art's parents – both of us having escaped the Nazis and made new lives in the United States.

Art is active in the Jewish community – always giving back, as so many of us who survived the Holocaust feel we need to give back and thank God for our survival and success in the United States of America. Art is a good man and I'm proud that he came to Beaver Street after he and his parents retired from their food store business.

Art Pollan
Executive Sales

This is my 33rd year at Beaver Street Fisheries, but I've known the Frisch family since I was five years old. My parents, Daniel and Helene Pollan, were in Auschwitz Concentration Camp and were liberated. The first chance we got, we came to this country, sponsored by the Jacksonville Jewish Center. My family had a little grocery business called Banner Food Stores. Harry and Fred worked at their mother's fresh fish place and I worked at my parent's grocery store. I had to work on the docks for a year and a half before I went into sales. You can't sell anything you don't know anything about – and I didn't know fish – so I learned. That's why they've been so successful. What they do makes sense.

Harry is an intelligent man who thinks things out and never makes a decision without looking at all sides of the issue. He reminds me of an older Bill Gates. He understands how to maximize profitability – how to manage personnel and use their thought patterns and abilities to promote his company. You can say he's a businessman, but there has to be a certain understanding there, too.

Harry and Art Pollan – April 2018

One example of many: We always had personal things to talk about. I walked into his office one day and he was working on his calculator as we talked. After I initiated the conversation, he kept going back to his calculator. I finally asked him what he was doing. He said, number one, he was trying to figure out his gas mileage and then decide whether it would behoove him to buy a year younger car to save on gas. He soon discovered he could save 11 cents a gallon by upgrading to a newer car. He not only took care of my opportunity (I call them opportunities, not problems), but he made a decision on a car, and ordered the two motors he needed for downstairs in the warehouse. He is a master of multi-tasking.

The man is 95 years old and still puts in more hours than most of us do. He leads a very plain life and puts his heart, soul and thoughts into this company. He never took any money out of this business personally, and nobody does a better job of giving back to his community. Harry is the epitome of what a gentleman should be. That's why people like him are so successful – they have humility and honor.

* * * * *

Dennis Kah is our head meat cutter at Beaver Street. He does the meat cutting for HF Outstanding Meat Products – Choice cuts of meat that are U.S. Certified Angus Beef – the very best! I remember that John Peyton, former mayor of Jacksonville, said that when he got some steak from us, it was the best steak he ever tasted.

Dennis Kah

Head Meat Cutter

I've been with Beaver Street Fisheries for 35 years, and I'm proud of the U.S.D.A.-inspected meat we sell here. This is truly like working for family. I'll never forget the day, a few decades ago, when I was leaving for vacation

Lloyd Carter and Dennis Kah- April 2018

and Ms. Lilo slipped a $100 bill in my hand and said, 'Have a nice time on your vacation.' Ms. Lilo was always generous with all of us. We knew she cared.

* * * * *

Speaking of $100 bills, I have a long-standing rule that just about everybody at Beaver Street knows by now. When we have a first-time visitor, I place a $100 bill on the table in my private conference room and introduce them to one of my trusted employees to give them the tour of our company. I tell our visitor that this $100 bill is theirs if they find one scrap of paper on the floor in our facility, and if they collect the $100, I will have the head of the person who conducted the tour. That person is usually Lloyd Carter, and as of April 2018, when he gave a tour to my guest, Nadine Gramling, Lloyd was still wearing his head.

Roger Denmark
R & D Manager

I've been here twenty-five years. I was 19 years of age when I came to work and now I have five kids, ages 11 to 25. Mr. Harry has blessed me beyond measure. He's a magnet – pulls you in.

Roger Denmark and Harry

I remember when I first got here, I didn't know anything. I had to learn everything. When I worked in the PQF – Public Quick Freeze – there was the full body of a small alligator in one of the freezers. It was in there as a joke, but it surprised me every time. One thing that was important to me was that when we sold to Sysco, there were no jobs lost – they honored our tenure. This is a family-oriented company and I'm so glad to be here.

* * * * *

Adam Husney
National Sales

Adam Husney & Harry

I started work here in 1983 at almost 21 years old in the night crew in the warehouse. I came to Harry Frisch and said, "Hey, I graduated from high school and I don't have much to offer, but I want to work here." He said he'd give me a chance. He's always been like a father figure to me – yelled at me a lot. Back in the day, he didn't like the clothes I wore. "Adam, come here!" he said. He had the guys who do uniforms give me some pants and shirts to wear to the office. He had a lot to do with who I am today.

I've worked my way through almost every department here – now I'm in the sales side of it. I've been here for so long – it feels like family. I'm 56 now.

Once, they moved me into the accounting department and I was looking over invoices when our sales manager, Leo, couldn't get his key to work in the door. He started kicking the door to open it and I offered to help. I kicked the door open. Harry called me into his office an hour later and said, "What did you do to that door?" I explained that I was helping Leo and he said, "If Leo jumped off the building, would you jump, too? Don't ever do that again!"

I was young and Harry Frisch was very much a hands-on involved teacher. He imparted great wisdom to me. There were *two things that would make him crazy – if he saw you walk past a piece of trash on the floor or if your phone rang twice and you didn't answer it … Pick up your trash and pick up your phone!*

Back in those days, everybody's job was everything. We did everything. That was his third pet peeve – if anybody had the nerve to say "that's not my job," it was all over for them.

Harry and Fred fought like crazy but they loved each other. When they started talking in German or Yiddish – that was when they were really mad!

One day I had on a pair of jeans with a hole in them. He yelled at me for 15 minutes. Harry only fired me once, though. I ran late on a Saturday morning. He called my house at 9 a.m. and I hadn't even left yet. He said, "This is Harry and my time clock says I have to fire you. Bye bye." There were no excuses – you had to be there, and the worst part was that he was always there first. He rehired me but I was never late again. Harry is like the Ever Ready Bunny – he never stops. He's always been a lead-by-example man. He ran a tight ship and he still does. He taught me about being family-oriented and now I try to be there for the ones coming up in the company – like he was for me.

* * * * *

One of the greatest blessings in my life today is when employees come to me and thank me. The older I get, the more often this happens, and those gestures mean a lot. Recently, Jeff Parisi, who's been with Beaver Street Fisheries since 1984, brought me a copy of an employment sheet I had written up when I hired him. He's kept it all these years. It had many hours listed on it that I expected him to work, and more times if needed. He told me it was the best thing he ever did in his life. The letter and a copy of the memo I sent regarding his training follow:

BEAVER STREET FISHERIES, INC.
P.O. BOX 41430 • JACKSONVILLE, FLORIDA 32203-1430
PHONE: (904) 354-5661

Telex: 56240
ANSBX: Frisfood Jax.
Cable: Beaverfish

March 12, 1984

Subject: Jeff Parisi

The following conditions of employment, with Beaver
Street Fisheries, Inc., have been discussed and
agreed upon by Jeff Parisi and myself.

1. The average work day is from 7:00 A.M. to 6:00 P.M.
and one-half day on staurday.

2. Under certain circumstances, a day could start earlier
and finish later.

3. Jeff will have the opportunity for full extensive
training and learning while working full time in all
area's of the warehouse, freezers, dry area's, shipping,
receiving, order entry, etc., as determined from time to
time.

4. His beginning compensation will be $295.00 weekly
and is to be reviewed after a period of 60 days.

Harry Frisch

Jeff Parisi

Producers • Distributors • Import • Export

Full Line of Food Products

MEMORANDUM

TO: HARRY SALISBURY   RUDY JOHNSON
            RANDY GUENTHER   JEAN BOWMAN
            GREG MAGRIPLIS   SAM ROGOZINSKI
            LEE PHILLIPS   CARLOS SANCHEZ
            JIM RUSHING   JOE LANG
            MIKE PINSON   JIM WATSON
            LORI WATKINS   KEN GRANT
            DAVID STEINFELD   TROY GREEN

FROM: BILL POLMANTEER

DATE: MARCH 12, 1984

SUBJECT: ORIENTATION & TRAINING OF JEFF PARISI

MR. JEFF PARISI JOINED THE COMPANY, EFFECTIVE MARCH 12, 1984. DURING
THE REMAINDER OF THIS WEEK AND A PORTION OF NEXT WEEK, JEFF WILL BE
MOVING FROM AREA TO AREA TO ACQUAINT HIMSELF WITH OUR OPERATIONS.
PLEASE REFER TO THE FOLLOWING SCHEDULE AND IN THE TIME ALLOTTED,
KINDLY PROVIDE JEFF WITH AS MUCH INFORMATION ABOUT YOUR PARTICULAR
OPERATION AS POSSIBLE.

TUESDAY, MARCH 13, 1984
NATIONAL SALES MEETING/7:00 A.M./MEETING ROOM
RANDY GUENTHER/9:00 A.M./SEA-EST SALES
GREG MAGRIPLIS/10:00 A.M./SEA-EST PRODUCTION
LEE PHILLIPS/12:30 P.M./FISHHOUSE
JIM RUSHING/2:30 P.M./P.Q.F. FREEZERS

WEDNESDAY, MARCH 14, 1984
MIKE PINSON/7:30 A.M./CREDIT
LORI WATKINS/8:30 A.M./CONTROL CENTER
DAVID STEINFELD/10:00 A.M./PURCHASING
RUDY JOHNSON/12:30 P.M./INVENTORY CONTROL
JEAN BOWMAN/2:30 P.M./P.Q.F. OFFICE

THURSDAY, MARCH 15, 1984
SAM ROGOZINSKI/7:30 A.M./ISLAND SEAFOOD
CARLOS SANCHEZ/9:30 A.M./NATIONAL SALEAS
JOE LANG/12:30 P.M./LOCAL SALES

FRIDAY, MARCH 16, 1984
LOCAL SALES MEETING/7:30 A.M./MEETING ROOM
KEN GRANT/10:30 A.M./LOCAL SHIPPING

SUNDAY, MARCH 18, 1984
TROY GREEN/8:00 P.M./NIGHT SHIFT LOADING

TUESDAY, MARCH 20, 1984
KEN GRANT/7:00 A.M./DELIVERY

Carlos Sanchez has been with us for 42 years and his knowledge of the seafood business is second to none. He is one of my most valued employees. Carlos, his dad and his uncle escaped to Miami from Castro's Cuba and opened a lobster processing plant called Florida Caribe Fisheries, but they lost their fishing boat, the Freskito, and their business due to lack of funds. We bought the company for a song in 1964 and made Florida Caribe Fisheries one of our subsidiaries. Carlos was just a kid back then, working at the plant in Miami. I didn't meet him until the early 1970's, after we sold Florida Caribe Fisheries. What happened was that some drug dealers approached the guy who was running the processing plant in the Keys and asked him to help with some night deliveries of what they called "square grouper" (Marijuana bales). Fred and I couldn't have that! We decided right away that the prudent thing would be to sell the company. Before long, Carlos was working full-time at Beaver Street here in Jacksonville. Carlos says I'm the one who made him so smart about seafood:

Carlos Sanchez

In the late 70's, Harry asked me to start teaching some of the local sales people about seafood, since I'd had experience working at the processing plant and all. He asked me to put on a seafood class every Friday morning and at the time I thought it was for the benefit of the sales people. I had no clue he was actually grooming me. In order to teach the class, I had to go to the library and do research on all species of fish since we were selling seafood from all over the world. By teaching that class, I learned, and that was his intent. He was grooming me to go into the sales department and then into the purchasing department. He's always got a plan and he is extremely forward thinking.

For instance, in 1977, he had me start our Quality Assurance Department, checking every shipment that came in and went out and giving him a report. At that time in the industry, there were

Carlos Sanchez and Harry

only two companies conducting Quality Control – Red Lobster and Beaver Street. Anything he did today was strategic thinking for tomorrow because in 1997, when the Food and Drug Administration began their Hazard Analysis Critical Control Point (HACCP) program, we were way ahead of the mandate. Today, in order to operate a seafood processing plant, you have to have at least one HACCP-certified employee – we have between 30 and 35 people with HACCP certification.

Harry treasures people who are straight with him. A defining moment in our relationship was when I first started working here and I snuck out to breakfast across the street at the Farmer's Market. He caught me sneaking in the back door and he confronted me, "You're sneaking in back door because you went out for breakfast," he said, expecting me to lie or make excuses. "Yes sir," I told him. "You're right." After that, he knew he could always count on me to tell him the truth.

My Dad, Carlos Sanchez, Sr., and my Uncle Ray brought a lot of experience in the lobster processing business to the table from growing up with it in Cuba. There are many intricacies involved in doing it properly. Dad and Fred Frisch traveled throughout the Caribbean purchasing lobster and now Ben has Tropic Seafood in the Bahamas.

Something unique about this company is that the Frisch's have always given all of their employees the opportunity to rise to their *full potential. They don't look at your education, ethnicity, religion, gender – in fact, Harry is almost myopic and focuses on one thing – your willingness to work hard and do your best. If you give him the effort, he will give you the chance to rise in the ranks.*

* * * * *

BSF Retirees ...

Although I, Harry Frisch, have no plans to retire, there are some much younger men than I who have chosen to retire from Beaver Street Fisheries. A couple of them were quite instrumental in helping make us what we are today, so I am giving them their say in this book:

Jim O'Brien
BSF Retired General Manager

I first interviewed with Harry in February of 1992 and got put to work in the first week of March of 1992. His interview style was interesting. He told me "young man, I see you've held a lot of positions in your life." I was 39 and I had been Director of Operations for the Florida Dairy Farmers Association and Director of Labor Relations for a trucking company. He told me I was going to have to work at every job in the building before he let me be a manager at Beaver Street. "You have to earn that," he said.

He put me on the night crew, day crew, cleaning crew, switchboard operator, floor sweeper, toilet cleaner – every menial task in the building – I was what he referred to as a manager trainee for three years. I never appreciated what he was doing for me until my later years. I learned a great deal doing those jobs – there was a great wisdom in what he had me do. I remember we were sitting in the interview and he said, "Where do you picture yourself in five years?" His general manager was sitting next to him at the time. I said, "In five years, I'll have his job." Harry laughed and said, "You got some chutzpah, buddy." That was my hiring story.

We had many heavy discussions where we didn't agree on small things, but never out front. It gives you so much freedom as a manager when you can go in behind closed doors and speak your mind and have no repercussions – a true hearing-out of things. Harry never let his ego get in the way of the business. He didn't want anyone to let their ego take over. Park your ego at the door when you come into Beaver Street.

He was singularly the best teacher I've ever had. He had a seventh grade education but he came with a Ph.D in wisdom – a master's degree in human psychology. I was a Marine for eight years – right out of high school – worked and moved around the country. When I found Harry Frisch, I never took another job.

My father always told me, "One day you'll run into someone you want to make a business life with – just the way you find a wife – you'll find the right person in time." When I found Harry, I knew I'd found the right person. He's tough as nails but inordinately fair – as much as you can make things fair in business. He treated me better than anybody had ever treated me in my life outside of family.

He never called me Jim – he usually called me Mr. O'Brien. Everybody called him Harry – the janitor called him Harry, but he and I had a special relationship. Harry said we were more like brothers than father and son. He said, "I have two sons! You and I are like brothers, but you're my little brother!"

Harry has a rabbi story for every occasion. If I was supposed to learn about patience, or anything else, he would tell me a rabbi story. Every rabbi story had a moral.

Harry always said that if you have to ask whether something's right or wrong, you can bet it's wrong. Harry illustrated this by remarking that even a baby knows right from wrong. "They go over to the wall plug and before they touch it, they look back at you. They know."

Harry used to say, "Jim, if you need an answer right now, the answer is no. But give me time to think about it and I'll get back to you." He believed that unless there's a fire, you don't need to rush into a decision. Time is your friend when you're making a decision. Sometimes the problem actually does go away. Harry said, "The soup is never eaten as hot as it's cooked." That's an old Yiddish proverb. Nothing is on fire the way you think it is – cool off the soup before you eat it. Never deal with people when you're angry. If you do, you'll always make a mistake.

One of the great managerial lessons he used to tell me -God doesn't make junk. The first time I had a serious problem with an employee, he asked me what I thought we should do. I told him I didn't know what else to do but fire the man. Harry said, "Fire him? A monkey can fire a person. Don't be a monkey. That person needs a job. He didn't steal from us – he didn't come to work drunk and he wasn't selling drugs. If he didn't commit a crime, manage to find the right job for him. Put him in the right position to make sure he's successful. God doesn't make junk."

That stuck with me my entire life. I can't recall ever firing anybody. Firing is the ultimate failure of management. God doesn't make junk. How do you argue with that kind of wisdom?

Harry used to say if you give your most important decisions two days, you'll almost never make a critical error. But no matter how honest people are, you put them in a situation to make a bad decision and they might do it.

After Beaver Street Foods got sold to Sysco, a lot changed. Where we were at that time – Karl was running Beaver Street Foods – Ben was running the Bahamas – Harry oversaw all of it, but he and Fred were running Beaver Street Fisheries. Karl had driven the sales at BSFoods – did a magnificent job of driving the sales and everybody knew it. It was amazing. They were competing with Sysco Foods – Walter Rudisilar, the President ... and in those days, Karl always had the upper hand – the best steaks, seafood – he had the best of everything. In customer service, there was nobody better than Karl. People loved him. His sales force loved him and he loved them back. It was a special group. In the spring of 1997, we were bursting at the seams. There was no room for growth at Beaver Street. We were looking at where we were going to move. Possibly, to buy property on the west side of town. We didn't know what we were going to do.

The opportunity came up to sell BSFoods to Sysco. We completed that deal in May/June of 1997 and part of Harry and Karl's deal was that Sysco had to take all 178 employees – guarantee their seniority – that was the deal – 100% of the employees – even after 25 years of seniority. It was an enviable position for longevity and pension at Sysco. Then we were left with just the export and seafood division. I can tell you we went from bulging at the seams to wondering how we were going to fill the space.

Sysco had agreed to start buying seafood from BSFisheries and they became the second biggest food service provider of choice – all the hotels, restaurants, hot dog stands, schools – in 200 area miles of Jacksonville. Paper goods, 1600 different items – immense – from hard-boiled eggs to artichoke hearts ... we had been Exports/Foods/Fisheries ... now Fisheries and Exports just exploded. Over the next five years, they went crazy. We had so much room to buy large quantities in advance – we were extremely competitive.

I was Tonto to Harry's Lone Ranger. Lathun Brigman and Harry were best friends. Lathun had been there longer than I was – before and after me – he's always been there – the trusted right hand of Harry. Precision and price ... the story behind the numbers – not just an accountant – an operations guy and an accountant! Lathun was the guy that was closest to Ben, Karl and Harry – very trusted.

Harry has the ability to speak with kings and commoners - make them all his best friends. He can talk to the janitor for twenty minutes. Karl and Harry love to entertain. Karl is fun-loving and sincere. He's as dear a person as you'll meet. He

Jim O'Brien and Karl Frisch

adored his sales force. It broke his heart when we sold Foods, but he knew it was the right thing for the organization and the family. He worked in Fisheries for a good long time. He initiated the IT projects – brought along the IT guys - he brought us into the 21st century – that was a huge deal – transforming the company. Karl laid the groundwork. Harry and Fred weren't computer savvy. Karl had to oversee that – be involved in that and keep his fingers on the pulse. When I first started there, we were still writing orders on paper. Karl worked with the IT people – automated everything – ran inventory on 5 x 7 index cards – we were right in that transition of moving from paper to computers. Karl was at the front of that – fearless when it came to looking at technology – loved the excitement that technology brought to the table. He made it happen.

* * * * *

Henry Lawrence Wiles (Bubba)

I was hired in 1980 to run the operations downstairs – refrigeration, maintenance, shipping, production areas. I'm a licensed refrigeration man. Mr. Harry oversaw the salesmen and the upstairs folks and I ran downstairs. It was a small operation and they didn't have a lot of money to work with, so I was it.

Local business was good back then. If we had a shipment to send out and no truck was available, Mr. Harry put it in a cab. He didn't believe in telling the customer no. That wasn't his philosophy. He never borrowed money to build anything – if he didn't make it – he didn't build it.

My daddy was a registered land surveyor. I could draw and survey and Mr. Harry liked that because he had to see things on paper. I drew enough drawings over the years for Mr. Harry that he would be able to walk to my house in socks on those drawings and never get them dirty – and I live in Mandarin – 35 miles from Beaver Street! I remember I drew up a picture of what we could do with the Farmer's Market – and look at it now!

About the second day I worked for Mr. Harry, he called me upstairs and said, "I need a favor. My wife still runs the little retail store down the road. Make me a promise – whatever that lady wants, make sure you do it for her. If she's down there and she's happy, she won't be up here trying to tell me what to do."

I always tried to make sure Mrs. Frisch was happy.

I loved Mrs. Frisch and she loved me too. One thing about her – by 11 o'clock in the day, if they opened the business, she would check the money and if they had a good bit of money, she took it out of the cash register and left them a little bit. She'd count the money – take it out – they couldn't rob the place. She was Johnny on the spot – she made sure it was thoroughly counted and she worked hard like everybody else.

My son, Chris, came to work about 1983 on the maintenance end of the business – he and Kenny Higgenbotham. They were just kids, right out of high school. Through the company, I sent them to refrigeration classes. They went there for four years – got their licenses – took the city tests and passed. They had to have the same degrees I had. Chris worked in all the production, meat room, seafood -he rebuilt the refrigeration. We didn't sub anything out to anybody – we covered everything ourselves.

I retired about 3 ½ years ago. My son is smarter than I was. He's the R & D Manager. Sets up these machines – knows what the capacity is – he's the backbone.

Mr. Fred was the kind of guy who said what was on his mind if you liked it or not. A lot of people didn't like Mr. Fred when he sometimes spoke out of turn. Mr. Fred ran our Nassau office with Ben Frisch. Back in 2001 or 2002, we built a brand-new plant over there. I spent about a year setting up the production for them. I was familiar with our set-up – Mr. Fred went about looking places over – he was never locked down like Mr. Harry.

One thing about Mr. Harry – he took care of his people. He might work you seven days a week, but you always got a Christmas bonus from Mr. Harry. He never let anybody do without on Christmas – even the temporaries.

Karl Frisch ran the local business – center of the plate – supplied people all over Jacksonville. That was his number one job. When we built the new freezer by Mr. Frisch's office, we built that for local business but by that time, our national business was our most profitable business.

Mr. Harry took extreme good care of me. The words out of his mouth: "Bubba, if you need something – here's a phone. You've got my number, call me." I was a poor boy. He increased my pay every year. He was always giving people credit – like my son, Chris – and like me. He complimented me until my head was bigger than my hat. I retired from there and they had a party – they gave me all kinds of compliments. I'd been there a long time and what I learned in 36 years – you don't have to have a college degree to build an empire – all you have to have is the desire and show people respect. You've got a man named Harry Frisch who built an empire on desire and hard work.

Ten tsdaka be'sever panim yafot u'be'simcha.
Give charity graciously and cheerfully.

CHAPTER TEN: Mitzvahs

SHAD KHAN AND HARRY FRISCH

Harry Frisch and Shad Khan share a common bond that comes from their incredible stories of coming to the United States as immigrants with very little and now being two of the most influential leaders in Jacksonville.

Their common values of a commitment to family, democracy, free-enterprise and hard-work are what brought them to where they are today. They have also both supported people in-need through their charitable endeavors, with a particular emphasis on education and vocational training.

Harry Frisch had very little formal education and as such, he places a special value on affording others the education and training they need for success in their professional lives. Harry often says "real life" practical education is so important, and he has spent an enormous part of his life mentoring professionals to apply the knowledge they learned in school within the work environment. He has also mentored countless political leaders, encouraging them to apply their political skills in service to their community.

Shad Khan's father and mother sacrificed for their son to receive the best education he could obtain in Pakistan. Realizing that he could not receive the higher education he needed in Pakistan, he was able to receive a scholarship to study at the University of Illinois. That opportunity has inspired Shad to provide support and scholarships to other worthy students over the years.

Beyond the importance of education, the importance of character is paramount for both Harry and Shad. Particularly for youth, they both emphasize the moral values of absolute respect for others, self-discipline, hard-work, determination, and stress the need to avoid peer pressure that leads to making poor choices.

A Mitzvah is a good deed according to God's Commandments. I believe in doing good deeds because God commands it and because so many people have helped me in my life that I want to help others.

Shad Khan, owner of the Jacksonville Jaguars NFL Football Team, is a man who does many mitzvahs as well. We share many of the same facts of life - the hard times and the hard work it took for each of us to get where we are today. Shad and I both came to the United States without means and both of us have reached respectable levels of means through determination and hard work.

We have a small foundation now – partnering with the Jaguars. Recently, I attended a Jaguars Foundation luncheon and, there it was announced that Harry Frisch was an honored guest. People applauded. Here I am – formerly a poor Jewish immigrant, now an honored guest who used to own two skybox suites at the Stadium where the Jaguars play their football games, but this year we decided to reduce it to one.

At the Foundation luncheon in August 2017, I sat at the same table with the Jacksonville Jaguars Quarterback Blake Bortles. We got to be good friends. I put my arm around him and told him that would bring him good luck. The Jaguars won their first game, too! They lost their second one, though. I think I need to put my arm around the quarterback and all the other team members next time. A young lady got a scholarship at that luncheon and we had a picture taken with Blake Bortles. It was my great pleasure to be honored like that. It means a great deal to me.

It's that kind of thing – a young scholarship recipient who wants to have her picture taken with me, the announcement at a big luncheon that they are privileged to have Harry Frisch there, getting to sit with the Jaguars Quarterback, helping bring a fine theater back and helping a friend reach a goal – it's that appreciation and recognition and satisfaction that makes a man feel good about what he's done in life.

At the Playoff Game in January of 2018 between the Jaguars and Steelers, I presented Shad Khan with a special New Years' present – a crisp $2 bill, a golden dollar coin with a wish for a Happy New Year from Harry Frisch.

When I gave it to Shad, I told him this was my good luck New Year Gift for him. I told him it's got to bring good luck because everything I put my arms around brings good luck. He said that if it worked, he would frame my gift! It worked! I plan to give him another New Year Gift in 2019! Maybe it will help the Jaguars get to the Super Bowl!

Speaking of golden dollars and philanthropy, I always give a few golden dollars (coins) to friends who are going to the Holy Land and I ask them to give them to poor people. God protects carriers of charity and I want God to protect my friends. People like it when I do that. I gave Thora some golden dollars – a little pouch – to take with her when she went home to visit her family in Iceland – she loved every minute of it and I know God protected her and brought her home. She came to Lilo and me 27 years ago, and I depend on her to take good care of me now.

* * * * *

Alhambra Dinner Theatre

Why did I want to save it? I know how it feels to have something special and lose it. I love Jacksonville and Jacksonville had to have a dinner theater. Also, I helped my friend Tod Booth have a light at the end of the tunnel.

I offered to help Tod Booth when he was about to lose the Alhambra a few years ago, but he called to say he was so broke he couldn't take me up on my offer ... he said he couldn't afford to serve anyone a cup of coffee. He'd had to sell his boat and other things just to keep from being bankrupt. Tod was my good friend and it hurt me to see him like that. It also hurt to think of losing our town's oldest dinner theater.

I knew Craig Smith from exercising at Epping Forest and I remember that Craig had a limousine service over on the beach and once told me that I could call him and he would take me anywhere anytime, free of charge! Craig came to me and asked me if I would give him the same offer I had given to Tod Booth for the Alhambra, and I said yes, as long as Tod Booth always had a place there. Craig took the deal and he has done a great job of bringing it back to life. Tod Booth called me recently to say he bought a new boat. That brought tears to my eyes.

Craig Smith, Harry Frisch and Nadine Gramling

At an intimate dinner party in March of 2018, my friend Craig Smith and I had a great time with a new friend, Nadine Gramling, who is a property owner and businesswoman in Jacksonville. Craig told Nadine all about how I helped him buy the Alhambra Dinner Theater and how, without me, it would not be in business today. He said, "Harry Frisch is one of the smartest men I've ever known. One day, I was sitting in his office at Beaver Street and he got a phone call from Europe and started speaking in fluent French! I had no idea he could speak so many languages until that day!"

On the big 50th Anniversary party for the Alhambra Dinner Theater,

Craig Smith called me up on the stage and told the packed house that I was the reason they were all there! It was a great honor. There is now a Harry Frisch Garden out in front of the Alhambra!

"Our garden is named in honor of Harry Frisch as a thank you for his dedication to the arts and theater in Jacksonville. Without him, the Alhambra would not have persevered to this day. Had it not been for Harry Frisch, owner of Beaver Street Fisheries and 50-year patron of the Alhambra, by now the theater would surely be a distant and fleeting memory."

"Frisch's continuing support of the Alhambra was absolutely essential," Craig Smith says. *"Without it, we couldn't have gotten off the ground."*

The Alhambra's iconic garden was dedicated to Harry Frisch on December 11th, at the theater's 50th birthday bash, in honor of his contributions to this theater, to the arts and, as a result, to the city of Jacksonville.

* * * * *

St. Johns River Taxi

Matt Schellenberg, Jacksonville City Council,
remembers the way it happened...

I had just had lunch with Harry at Two Doors Down. He was reading the Financial News and Daily Report and noticed the River Taxi was going out of business. Harry said, "I think we need to have a taxi on the river." I agreed. I went back and read the article about the city shutting down the river taxi and I called him back. "We need to do something," I said. He responded. "Let's find some pontoon boats and get somebody to operate them. Sightseeing boats."

By coincidence, I knew a guy near Orlando that had a couple of them for sale. I had to go down to Orlando for business and I called him up and asked if he had those boats available. He did. He said the engines needed some work. I found out how much money it would take to get them operational and I called Harry. I said, "This is the deal. He has them and he's ready to go if you have an interest." Harry said, "Make it happen."

The Orlando man was Robbie Cunningham. He trusted me, and he trusted Harry – he fulfilled all of Harry's obligations. We found somebody to operate them and Harry worked with the City on the deal. All Harry asked was to be reimbursed. He didn't want to make any money on the deal at all. It was for the City. It was up and running within about 90 days. Startling, really. I remember going to the dock and seeing the pontoon boat with Harry and his son, Ben. Harry was ecstatic because he cares so much about this city. He is a giving, loving person.

An article about Harry and the River Taxi ran in the August 2014 edition of the *Resident Community News*. The article, written by Editor Kate Hallock, who also took the photographs, is reprinted from the *Resident Community News* below:

Frisch takes on Water Taxis
Prominent leader steps up

In spite of Harry Frisch's good intentions, the City of Jacksonville doesn't seem to be any further along with resolving the issue of water taxi service. When the second pontoon boat, seating 100 passengers, was delivered early in July, Frisch came out to Sadler Point Marina to look at his purchases.

He was, in typical fashion, modest about his efforts to keep water transportation alive in downtown Jacksonville.

"I'll tell you, it's not [just] helping out the City, it's helping out myself, my family, my friends, the business and everything in Jacksonville," he said. "I like to do things that everybody says is impossible. Give it to me."

Frisch, who came to the United States six decades ago, has a fondness for Jacksonville voiced by many transplants to the area. "I'm here in Jacksonville over 60 years and didn't have very much when I came here. Jacksonville has been very good to me and it was important to give back."

Harry Frisch, founder of Beaver Street Fisheries, at the delivery of the 100-passenger water taxi at Sadler Point Marina.

He also sees the city's potential for greatness.

"I'm kind of selfish about it," Frisch stated. "I'm telling you right now, four or five years from now, with the Jaguars and all the other good things that are happening, Jacksonville will be the finest city in the United States. You can take that to the bank."

He's a huge supporter of Shahid Khan, owner of the Jacksonville Jaguars, and wants to do his part in attracting visitors to the city. "People from the whole world will come to visit us. You have a man there with vision and the money to support it," Frisch said, speaking of Khan. When Brooks Busey, owner of Sadler Point Marina, came out to meet Frisch and thank him for his help in keeping the water taxis in Jacksonville, the San Jose/Beauclerc resident shrugged it off.

"Someone had to do it; it was important for Jacksonville. Some logistics didn't work properly and it was made a big issue when it didn't need to be. We didn't want the boats to get away," Frisch said. "Too bad they weren't running for Fourth of July, but better late than never."

"Robbie Cunningham, owner of Trident Pontoons, Harry Frisch and Ben Frisch of Beaver Street Fisheries, and District 6 Councilman Matt Schellenberg in front of the 100-passenger water taxi delivered early last month to Sadler Point Marina.

This isn't the first time that Frisch has done something for Jacksonville with little to no expectation of return. When he founded Beaver Street Fisheries, he soon realized that something was missing and did something about it.

Robbie Cunningham, owner of Trident Pontoons, Harry Frisch and Ben Frisch of Beaver Street Fisheries, and District 6 Councilman Matt Schellenberg in front of the 100-passenger water taxi delivered early last month to Sadler Point Marina.

"The Farmer's Market is not a profit for us, but Jacksonville has to have a farmer's market." That is also true of the water taxi service, according to Frisch. "Jacksonville without a water taxi wouldn't be Jacksonville."

As of press time, both water taxis were still sitting up on blocks in the boatyard on the Ortega River, awaiting Coast Guard inspection and certification, a temporary operator and a permanent owner. Although it was a sweltering day when Native Choice was delivered, Frisch wanted to see his taxis. "I'm all excited to see them. It's like a dream come true."

* * * * *

There are so many other places that have the Frisch name on a plaque or are named after the Frisch family. My sons and grandsons have carried on with the philanthropy through giving to important causes and institutions like the JCA and River Garden and, in December of 2017, my son Ben represented our family at the ribbon cutting for the new Frisch Family Holocaust Museum located within the new Alan J. Taffet Building which now houses Jewish Family and Community Services (JFCS). Ben was quoted in the Resident Community News article as saying, "The Holocaust should never have happened and never be forgotten. We will continue to give our support for many years to come as our family's remembrance of Lilo and Harry Frisch, both of whom are Holocaust survivors."

My friend, Laurie DuBow, challenged guests to remember what event, conversation or person first stimulated them to give back. He said, "I distinctly remember my mother saying that there is always something you can give to those in need, and when you do, it benefits you as well as them."

Jacksonville sixth Florida city to establish Holocaust museum

The official ribbon-cutting was done by Laurie DuBow, Lori Leach, Colleen Rodriquez, Ben Frisch, Ina Taffet, Rabbi Yaakov Fisch, Kalilah Jamall, staff assistant, Office of U.S. Senator Bill Nelson, Essence McKinney, a child in JFCS's foster care services, JFCS volunteer Eunice Zisser, and Matthew Villeareal, a student in JFCS's Achievers for Life program.

* * * * *

Café Frisch

Wanda Willis, Associate Director of Development for Major Gifts at FSCJ ... tells the story of Café Frisch ...

The Frisch family – they are a wonderful family and a wonderful company as well. Thanks to Harry and Beaver Street Fisheries, the Culinary Department at FSCJ's downtown campus now has the Café Frisch on the campus on West State Street. We had an awesome committee on campus involved in putting the whole thing together. The Frisch Café is open on Tuesdays and Thursdays for lunch and Thursday evenings for dinner. The walls of the Café feature historic pictures from Beaver Street Fisheries as well as some of Harry Frisch's Points of Business. It is a wall mural with some of Harry Frisch's points of good business practice mounted on the wall on plates. "Center of the Plate" is important to the Frisch family.

Grand Opening of Café Frisch – Feb. 15, 2018 – Harry Frisch and Wanda Willis

Harry insisted on the café being named after the Frisch family – not just Harry. He's never been the kind of person who was showy – always humble with his philanthropic work, too. Only in the past couple of years has he allowed people to give him awards and accolades. For many years, he wouldn't even accept awards. I'm speaking from my heart when I say I love Mr. Harry. It's easy to speak from your heart about such a kind and gentle soul.

The grand opening of Café Frisch was on February 15, 2018 – it was a great day that was written up in several local newspapers including the Financial news and Daily Record:

Page 16 • Tuesday, February 20, 2018 • Financial News & Daily Record

A grand opening for Café Frisch

From left, Martha Barrett, Florida State College at Jacksonville President Cynthia Bioteau, Harry Frisch, Karl Frisch and Ben Frisch cut the ribbon to mark the grand opening Thursday of FSCJ's Café Frisch. The teaching café, made possible by a gift from the Frisch family, is at the FSCJ Downtown Campus at 101 W. State St. in Building C, Room 106. It is open 11:30 a.m.-12:30 p.m. Tuesday and Thursday and also has seatings at 6:30 p.m. and 7 p.m. Thursday. Lunch is $9 and dinner is $11, according to its website. Reservations are required. Call (904) 633-8151 or visit fscj.edu/cafe-frisch

More photos online at jaxdailyrecord.com

The *Resident Community News* also ran a nice piece in the March San Jose issue on the grand opening with the headline as follows:

San Jose resident funds café for FSCJ culinary arts students

Culinary students and staff at FSCJ's Culinary Arts and Hospitality Program outdid themselves on February 15, at the grand opening of Café Frisch, a simulated restaurant at the downtown campus designed to showcase their talents to the community.

Guest of Honor Harry Frisch, founder of Beaver Street Fisheries, and his sons, Ben and Karl Frisch, cut the ribbon at the door of the new restaurant made possible by the Harry Frisch family and the Beaver Street Foundation. Speaking at the ribbon-cutting

ceremony were Martha Barrett, FSCJ Foundation board chair, Dr. Cynthia Bioteau, FSCJ President, Connie Pecoraro, culinary student, Cleve Warren, FSCJ Foundation Executive Director, and Harry Frisch.

"We've been working hard on the appearance of this café as it was important to convey the great heritage of the Frisch family here in Jacksonville," said Wanda Willis, Director of Development of Major Gifts for the FSCJ Foundation.

Pointing out the unique photographic wall created from an old black and white 1950's Beaver Street Fisheries photo.

Harry Frisch with FSCJ Culinary Students at Café Frish
Feb. 15, 2018

As he sat at the table with me and enjoyed delicious cuisine prepared by the culinary students, my son, Ben Frisch, glanced at the wall photo and remembered riding in those same trucks with me and the men pictured there. I was impressed with the wall and when I saw another wall covered with dinner plates bearing some of my familiar points of good business practice, such as "Don't criticize your competitors," "Smile constantly," "Treat employees with respect," and "Use Your Head," interspersed with photos of me and my beloved Lilo, tears came to my eyes. "This is a great honor," I told the culinary students and staff as I posed in the doorway of the unique photographic wall mural of old Beaver Street Fisheries. It was a proud day for my sons, Karl and Ben, and for me.

Ben, Harry and Karl Frisch

It was also a delicious culinary experience for all present at the grand opening! The menu was like that of a fine restaurant and the food was perfectly prepared, with a delicious dessert following the main course.

I am my Beloved's אֲנִי לְדוֹדִי My Beloved is mine וְדוֹדִי לִי

CHAPTER ELEVEN: Lilo's Room

Lilo and Harry - 1950s

Beautiful Lilo Laughing

When my beloved Lilo became ill, I had a special room in our home designed just for her. It has high windows with screens that can be opened for fresh air and to let the sun shine in … she loved the sights and smells of the garden. I had a beautiful garden planted outside the windows, so she could sit in her recliner and look out and enjoy nature. There is a big-screen television in there and a big chair for each of us. Sadly, she never was well enough to use the room much, but I still call it "Lilo's room"

Lilo – Ready to Dance

and sometimes I just sit in there for a while and enjoy the fresh air and scent of flowers and think of the many wonderful years we spent together. Sixty-eight years we were married and there was never a night when we went to bed angry. There was never an argument in our home that involved four letter words. I had great love and respect for my wife and she had great love and respect for me.

We loved to dance. I was usually the first one out on the dance floor, but Lilo sometimes wanted to wait a little bit. Not me!

Chief Leonard Propper of the Jacksonville Sheriff's Office calls Lilo "an angel of a lady." He talks about being so sad when she passed away and so thankful that Ben asked him to help with her funeral:

I decided I'd knock the rust off my motorcycle and lead the service from Mandarin to Arlington, but then I realized I could do better than that. The family didn't know I called my good friend Telis Assimenios, GM at Tom Bush BMW, and asked him for a big favor. I simply informed Telis that Ms. Lilo had passed away and I would like to have her picture and a memorial for her on that huge storefront sign of Tom Bush Toyota on Atlantic Blvd. between the hours of 9:30 and 10:30 a.m. so that the family would see it as I led the motor escort to the funeral home. He instantly agreed to do it. We stopped in front of the sign so the family could see it. I felt so blessed that a phone call to Telis made a wish a reality. Tom Bush is a family business like Beaver Street Fisheries is a family business – they have a similar philosophy, are 100 percent customer-oriented and generous with PAL (Police Athletic League), which is my passion. If every company was like Tom Bush and Beaver Street Fisheries, the world would be a better place.

Chief Propper further noted that he got "the sweetest, most heartfelt thankyou letter from Ben Frisch after Ms. Lilo's funeral that I've ever gotten in my career. Ben Frisch's letter was so personal that I shared it only with the sheriff."

Marty Goetz:

Lilo's illness was progressive – chronic – they both managed it well. Harry created a team – teams of caregivers – who over time became like family to him – there's no other way to put it. He looked to bring whatever resources Lilo needed into his home so that she could receive the care that he wanted her to have and so that he could be there with her. They were the quintessential love story – Harry and Lilo – I have some of the photos of them that are really sweet – this was a love story.

They were a wonderful couple – Lilo had a wicked sense of humor – you wouldn't have known it – she had no problem telling a dirty joke – Harry didn't either – but she would tell it better.

One thing that Harry said to me – Lilo was receiving care from River Garden's home health agency and Harry depended on us to be straight and honest with him on what she needed around care. At some point when she needed a different kind of bed to be more comfortable – and my doctor said she really needs to have this kind of bed – Harry called and asked me my opinion – did I think this was correct. I was honored. He made it clear that he wanted to provide her whatever she needed. He felt no sense of obligation to her – it was because he loved her so much. I remember being there when he would come home from work. Lilo was ill – the first thing he did was to come in, give her a kiss, sit down next to her, tell her about the day – and then he would bring me into the conversation. This man loved his wife from the day he met her until the day she died. There was not one day *he didn't adore her – this was a lifetime of love. Harry would say that Lilo was responsible for his success – she was with him the entire way- she constantly would say Use Your Head!*

Dr. Steve Wallace:

Lilo was an extraordinary person. I would describe her as someone having great quiet strength. She was quiet – very strong and steady in her approach to life – completely devoted to her family – had some real challenges early on as a young mother with young children – closing up their lives and moving to this place called Jacksonville, Florida. Lilo and Harry had an exemplary relationship – they were truly a team. Harry deeply valued and respected Lilo's views on things. Her quiet strength ran deep – you know she had been a Lieutenant in the Royal Air Force.

Lilo was an avid Jaguars fan. In the skybox, she liked to sit in one of the upholstered chairs and watch the game on the big screen television, and God help anyone who stood in front of her on a play. She was really serious … all these people milling around and talking – I got caught a couple of times. Lilo was laser focused on every play of the game.

Jim O'Brien:

Lilo Frisch. My first meeting with Lilo, I was chopping firewood for the smoker so she could smoke fish down at the fish store. As time went on, she became one of my mentors – she was like a mother to us all. She would stop and say hello to everyone when she came into the warehouse. If you had gained any weight, Lilo would tell you that you needed to lose weight. She would tell you to take echinacea (natural remedy) if you had a cold. She never wasted anything – she always made sure you were taken care of. If we had food that could be sent to the food bank she wanted to make sure it got there in a proper manner. We'd have dented cans, overstock – perfectly good and useful, but you can't sell them – a torn bag of flour – these things certainly made someone happy at Clara White Mission or the St. Francis Soup Kitchen. Lilo and Karl made sure nobody in the community went hungry if they could help it, including the Sulzbacher Center for the Homeless. They made sure we were a good corporate partner with the community. The family never forgot where they came from.

Lilo and Harry taught Ben and Karl the old ways. They never forgot. Something to be admired about Lilo. She always had a kind word for everybody. She was a dear woman. I was away when she passed. It was a definite heartbreak for everyone who knew her. I was sorry not to be there. She was very proud of her service to the military in Israel. She talked to me about it a lot, knowing I'd been in the Marine Corps. We felt a camaraderie about our times in service.

Lilo had a closet filled with clothes. She loved to shop, but she never paid full price for anything. She'd call the manager and ask him when an item would be on sale. Usually, because she was such a good customer, the manager would say, "For you, I'll put it on sale now."

Hadassah wanted me to give them an endowment, but I don't believe in endowments. I contribute to Hadassah because they helped Lilo as a girl and they were important to her all her life, but I won't establish an endowment. An endowment makes a commitment after my death – I want my sons to have their choice on their charities.

Lilo's favorite flower was a Gerbera Daisy.

Thora Rose, Housekeeper for 27 years:

Mrs. Frisch found my ad in the paper and she called me. My ad said "European Housekeeper." I had several calls but she was the only who wanted to hire me four days a week. I met them at Piccadilly Cafeteria at Regency Square. When I saw them walking toward me, I thought, "I know this couple. This is Mr. and Mrs. Frisch." Mrs. Frisch told me later that she turned to Mr. Harry when she saw me and said, "That's Thora."

I'm from Iceland. My husband and I lived in New York and he decided to retire here. He died 24 years ago, after I had started working for the Frisch's in 1990. Mrs. Frisch and I made a great team.

She would come home and say, "Thora, we've got to make a pot of soup." I'd say, "Where's the recipe?" There was no recipe. All of her ingredients were fresh and she might have as many as 18 ingredients for a pot of soup.

Mrs. Frisch had learned how to stretch meals for a family of four. She talked about how she would go the market and buy two chickens. She'd boil them first to get the broth. Then she'd cut the meat off the breast because no one wanted the breast meat. She'd bake the chicken for one meal. She'd make chicken meatballs from the white meat. Then she'd serve chicken soup.

She was way ahead of her time when it came to cooking and eating fresh and healthy. Mr. Frisch always joked that he couldn't recognize "all the strange things my wife has in the refrigerator." She had things like kale and cauliflower, and Cod Liver Oil and she always took a lot of vitamins. She was always teaching – trying to get people to eat new, healthy things. I'd say to her, "I know what it tastes like."

One time we had a whole bunch of ripe bananas. She never threw anything away. We must have made fifteen banana nut breads that day. We were always making cakes and cookies to give away. She said that she always made sure she got a job where she could eat – she had been through times when food was scarce.

Mrs. Frisch had a great sense of humor. She loved a good joke and a funny saying, like "The more you weigh, the harder you are to kidnap. Stay safe. Eat cake." She was very conscious of weight and wanted everyone, including me, to eat right and weigh light. She used to joke that calories are little creatures that hide in your closet and sew your clothes a little tighter every night.

She told me that when she was a girl of 14, she was sent to Berlin to be with a family just to see if she could be on her own and attend the Hadassah Agricultural School. Later, she joined the Royal British Air Force. When I asked her why she joined the Air Force, she answered, "Their uniforms were blue and I looked good in blue." She did look good in blue.

Mrs. Frisch loved clothes. We went shopping all the time for clothes and food. If there was a sale, we were there. Dillards, Belk, Beall's … she liked shopping at the Avenues. We were a great team. She was tough sometimes – wanted things done a certain way, but she was thankful for everything. She was getting close to retiring when they hired me. She retired at age 70 but she stayed busy. She was vivacious and full of energy – always on the go. She was like a mother to me – outspoken and always teaching. She would say what was on her mind. She enjoyed social gatherings and people wanted to be around her.

Mrs. Frisch drove until she was in her 80's. She would sometimes take her grandchildren for haircuts and shoes. She didn't go out to lunch much with friends, but we went everywhere together.

After she broke her wrist from a fall in late 2008, things went from bad to worse. She got a staph infection and was on medication for about six months. She also had Osteoporosis. Then in about 2009, she was diagnosed with Parkinson's Disease. Dr. Willis sent her to a neurologist. Her hands were trembling and she began shuffling when she walked. In 2011, I went to Iceland, but after that I stayed close by because she came down with a Parkinson's-related condition called Lewy Body Dementia.

Thora with Harry and Lilo – Etz Chaim event in 2015

When she got sick, nobody could have done more for his wife than Mr. Frisch did. He had people round the clock for her – bought her a special mattress. He loved her very much. During the last couple of years when she was so ill and had so many people in and out to care for her, they would say to me that they couldn't get her to respond; that she wasn't speaking anymore. That's when I would lean over and whisper in her ear, "Beautiful Lady, say Hi Ho," and she would smile and say, "Hi Ho."

She died August 19, 2016. I miss her.

Maria Mayo and Thora Rose with Harry and Lilo 2015

Maria Mayo, Caregiver for seven years:

Maria Mayo with Lilo on the porch

I was hired by the Human Resource Manager at Beaver Street after Miss Lilo's last hip surgery. She needed help with personal care. I live in Arlington – about 30 minutes away. I'm here six days a week from 2 p.m. until 8:30 p.m. and on Saturday mornings.

Miss Lilo taught me how to cook Butternut Squash Soup with Ginger. How to fix sweet potatoes, pureed with milk – and flounder. She would supervise me cooking.

She loved birds and flowers. When she was well, we would take a walk in the cul de sac and sit out on the porch drinking coffee and watching the birds. She taught me the names of flowers. She loved Gerber Daisies. She would have one cookie with her coffee – just one. I was embarrassed to have more than that in front of her. Miss Lilo was an easy person to love.

Martha Rothenberg:

Lilo was one of the kindest women – she was the most generous person – no matter what it took, if she couldn't do it, she would get others to do it. She was determined to get what she needed. A friend who needed money talked me into selling some little dessert plates and I asked Lilo if she wanted them – she said, "I don't need any plates, but I'll buy them." It was funny – her whole family saw to it that she had what she needed – she didn't need plates. I remember bringing her the plates. She bought them. She wasn't going to turn me down even though she needed the plates like she needed a hole in the head. Every time we bumped into each other, she'd smile and say, "Plates?"

Lilo and I were both at River Garden at the same time for quite a while. I had broken my hip and my pelvis at the same time, tripping over my dog, and I don't know what it was that took Lilo there that time, but she got out before I did. Sometimes, we'd eat meals together in the dining room and just chat about family and what was happening in the world. I wish I'd gone more out of my way to go see her when she was in her last

few years of life … we all get wrapped up in our own things and time slips by. I remember her fondly – how she loved her family and how she loved and served the Lord. Lilo was a good friend and a good woman.

* * * * *

Harry and Sandra Clayton, Caregiver

Today Thora Rose, Maria Mayo, and Sandra Clayton are with me at home to help me as efficiently as they helped Lilo. I am grateful for all of them.

Ereh iz Fil tei'erer far gelt.
Honor is dearer than money.

CHAPTER TWELVE: Honors, Awards & Tributes

Certificate of Appreciation

Junior Achievement
Jacksonville, Florida

On behalf of the people of the Third Congressional District of Florida it is my great honor to present this certificate to

Harry Frisch.

On this nineteenth day of April in the year two-thousand and twelve, we commend you as the 14th Annual Thompson S. Baker "SOLID AS A ROCK" honoree. You are a valuable resource and a role model to those who may follow in your footsteps. May you share your experiences and inspire others.

Corrine Brown
Member of Congress

April 19, 2012
Date

Introduced by Council Member Gaffney & Co-Sponsored by Council Members Hazouri, Carter, Schellenberg, Morgan, Anderson, Becton, Bowman, Boyer, Lopez-Brosche, K. Brown, R. Brown, Crescimbeni, Dennis, Ferraro, Gulliford, Love, Newby and Wilson:

RESOLUTION 2015-614-A

A RESOLUTION HONORING AND COMMENDING HARRY FRISCH FOR HIS LIFETIME OF SERVICE TO JACKSONVILLE

WHEREAS, Harry Frisch was born in Vienna, Austria in 1923, fled the incoming Nazi regime with his family in 1928 through Czechoslovakia to Palestine and, after running a successful auto repair shop in the new nation of Israel, immigrated to the United States in 1953 to reunite with his family who had moved to America several years earlier; and

WHEREAS, when he arrived in the Unites States, Mr. Frisch came to Jacksonville where his mother stepfather and brother had started a fish market on Beaver Street that over the years has grown into the Beaver Street Fisheries empire we know today; and

WHEREAS, through hard work, honest dealing and the application of good common sense, Harry Frisch and his parents, brother, sons and now grandchildren have grown the family's small business into an international seafood supplier, employing more than 400 people in the United States and in the Bahamas and shipping seafood and other foods and supplies across the country and around the world to more than 50 countries; and

WHEREAS, concurrent with his business success, Mr. Frisch has long been active in civic affairs and philanthropic endeavors, giving back to his adopted community through such ventures as the Jacksonville Farmer's Market that his company owns and operates as a vital community resource, his purchase and lease of two water taxis to the City to keep that vital service operating through change of operators, and through the Beaver Street Foundation which supports numerous not-for-profits serving the needs of the Jacksonville community; and

WHEREAS, Harry Frisch was presented the Thompson S. Baker "Solid As A Rock" award by Junior Achievement of North Florida in 2012 and was named to the First Coast Business Hall of Fame in 2014, and is deserving of additional recognition by the City of Jacksonville for his countless contributions to the city over the course of five decades; now therefore

BE IT RESOLVED by the Council of the City of Jacksonville:

The City of Jacksonville hereby honors and commends Harry Frisch for his decades of contributions to the economy and the civic life of Jacksonville. His example of hard work, honest dealing and civic spirit stand as a model for responsible leadership and corporate engagement, and the City wishes Mr. Frisch many more years of health, happiness and success.

ADOPTED BY THE COUNCIL
September 8, 2015

_____
Greg Anderson
Council President

ATTEST:

_____
Cheryl L. Brown
Council Secretary

**Adam. Mark, Harry, Karl and Steven –
Resolution from City of Jacksonville**

Frisch, Marlier honored at FSCJ commencement

Harry Frisch, center, and Jim Marlier were honored last week for the significant contributions they have made to Florida State College at Jacksonville. Frisch is founder of Beaver Street Fisheries and has been a longtime contributor to the school, including establishing the Frisch Institute for Senior Care. He attended the ceremony with his son, Karl, left, and received an honorary bachelor's degree from FSCJ board Chair Jimmie Mayo. Marlier, not pictured, received the distinguished alumni award. He graduated in 1969 and served on the FSCJ Foundation board of directors.

**Honorary Bachelor of Science Degree in Business Administration
Florida State College of Jacksonville Nov 13, 2017**

I was honored to be receiving an Honorary Bachelor of Science Degree in Business Administration from FSCJ ... for someone with a 7th Grade education, that's a nice compliment!

Harry Frisch flanked by his sons Ben (left) and Karl (right)

Icons of industry honored by Junior Achievement

Posted on December 4, 2017 By EditorNeighborhood News, RECENT NEWS

Nearly 200 friends and family members of Harry Frisch and W. W. "Bill" Gay were on hand Nov. 13 at UNF's Adam W. Herbert University Center to celebrate with them as they received Lifetime Achievement Awards from Junior Achievement of North Florida (JA).

Frisch, 94, and Gay, 91, are two Jacksonville icons of industry who have climbed the stairway of success during their lifetimes and shared that success generously with many in their community, including Junior Achievement of North Florida.

Chartered in 1963, with Gay a member of the founding board of directors, JA of North Florida promotes workforce readiness, financial literacy and entrepreneurship programs for students K-12. JA of North Florida has grown from reaching 225 students in 1963 to reaching 60,000 students this year.

Co-chairs Ronnie Fussell, Clerk of the Circuit Court, and Jeff Edwards, chief financial officer for Beaver Street Fisheries, both long-time supporters of JA, were credited with initiating the first-ever Lifetime Achievement Awards.

Harry Frisch and W.W. "Bill" Gay with Junior Achievement emcees Josh Miller, Michael Esguerra and Sabrien Bishop

Presenting the award to Gay, founder and CEO of W. W. Gay Mechanical Contractor, Inc., Fussell noted that Gay had been a major role model and mentor for him, and had tirelessly promoted and supported JA throughout his long career. Calling Gay an "institution" in North Florida, Fussell praised Gay's business acumen and philanthropy and his passion for helping children.

Jeff Edwards, who has been with Beaver Street Fisheries for 35 years, presented the Lifetime Achievement Award to Frisch, chairman of the board of Beaver Street Fisheries.

Describing Frisch's challenges in his native Vienna, Austria, and again in Palestine (now Israel), and again when he and his family immigrated to Jacksonville, Edwards talked of how Frisch has worked with four generations of his family for more than 60 years to build the business, and praised Frisch's philanthropy and generous support of countless community nonprofits, including JA of North Florida.

Reprinted with Permission - Resident Community News

February 3, 2018

Dear Guests, Colleagues and Friends,

Welcome to the 11th annual A Night for Heroes gala presented by Perry – McCall Construction, Inc. UF Health Jacksonville is honored to be home to one of Jacksonville's most valuable community assets, TraumaOne.

UF Health Jacksonville and TraumaOne are proud to serve the Northeast Florida and Southeast Georgia communities, providing lifesaving care to more than 4,000 trauma victims annually. It is our experience and expertise that makes us the region's leader in trauma care.

You are our valued partners in improving trauma care that impacts both patients and families. Tonight, I recognize each of you here as heroes and we thank you for your continued generosity. Your support throughout the years has allowed us to raise over $1.2 million to contribute to the critical needs of the trauma program. We would like to extend a special thank you to tonight's event sponsors — without you, this evening's success would not be possible.

The A Night for Heroes gala honors the men and women who care for trauma patients and their families each day; they are the true heroes in our community. Congratulations to each of the honorees and thank you for your dedication. We would also like to thank Robert and Claudia Ayer for joining us this evening and sharing their personal experience.

Tonight promises to be an inspiring and memorable event. Thank you for your contributions to TraumaOne and enjoy the evening!

Sincerely,

Leon L. Haley Jr., MD, MHSA
CEO, UF Health Jacksonville
Dean, University of Florida College of Medicine – Jacksonville
Vice President for Health Affairs, University of Florida

4   A NIGHT FOR HEROES /// LETTER FROM CEO

February 3, 2018

Dear Friends,

It is my pleasure to welcome you to the 11th annual A Night for Heroes gala.

It is an honor to support this special night as we celebrate our local heroes – the men and women in our community who care for trauma victims and support their families. The Frisch Family would like to congratulate each of tonight's honorees and extend our sincere appreciation for all of their hard work.

TraumaOne is an invaluable asset and we are thankful for the caliber of professionals who work at UF Health Jacksonville. Their dedication ensures that all of us have access to lifesaving care in case of traumatic injury. They make a real difference, as does your support and presence this evening.

We are committed to the success of UF Health Jacksonville and the vital role it serves in our community. Thank you for making your own commitment and for your generous support of this important community resource.

Best wishes for a wonderful evening!

Sincerely,

Harry Frisch

A NIGHT FOR HEROES /// LETTER FROM HONORARY CHAIR   5

Harry Frisch - Honorary Chairman – A Night for Heroes – Feb. 3, 2018

HARRY FRISCH
AT TORAH ACADEMY OF JACKSONVILLE

MAY, 2018

On May 29, 2018, I was honored by Torah Academy of Jacksonville at Etz Chaim Synagogue for my contributions to the school. I was able to visit the students earlier in the month and had a wonderful time with them. At one point, I spoke to them in Hebrew and they were surprised and, I think, delighted. I was then able to bless each child in turn as they came up to me and hugged me. It was a blessing both ways – for them and for me.

At the big Annual Dinner when I was honored, I asked that my family who were present come up to the stage and have a photograph taken with me because they are all so important to the man that I have become. It was a great honor.

**Honoree Harry Frisch & family members at Etz Chaim Synagogue's
Annual Dinner for Torah Academy of Jacksonville
Lighting the World - May 29, 2018**

During the last few years, I've received so many awards, it's hard to keep track of them all! A few of them are listed below, but the main thing I want to say is that the biggest honor I have had is the respect and love of my family and friends.

- **National Philanthropy Day, 2014- Harry and Lilo Frisch honored.**
- **First Coast Business Hall of Fame Induction by Florida Council on Economic Education November 20, 2014**
- **Service to Agriculture Award - Duval County Farm Bureau – Dec. 8, 2015**
- **ONE JAX HUMANITARIAN AWARD – Silver Medallion Honoree – May 5, 2016**

Besser tsen gutter freind aider ain soinch.
Better to have ten good friends than one enemy.

CHAPTER THIRTEEN: Ten Good Friends ... and Counting

In my 94 years, I've made many good friends, and I treasure them. My biographer contacted several of them and got quotes from them for this book. Here are a few:

Marty Goetz, CEO – River Garden

Marty Goetz and Harry

I've lived 39 years in Jacksonville and known Harry Frisch for decades. He has been a philanthropist for as long as I've known him. Harry is a champion for all of Jacksonville ... all the agencies ... whether Jewish or not.

For instance, when he got the river taxi, Harry's goal was not to get into the transportation business but to be supportive of the growth of this city. Harry sees Jacksonville's continued potential to be one of the great cities of America and he feels privileged to be part of it.

Harry came here with nothing and this was not his native language. He will tell you - and he takes a great deal of pleasure in saying it - that he has no formal education. It's a big mistake to think this guy will be easy – he is super smart. He thinks about things deeply. I've learned from him. Early on, he invited me to Beaver Street Fisheries for a tour and every member of his staff knew him and he knew their names. He has hundreds of employees. None of them were startled to see him walking around on the factory floor and he had a kind word for every one of them. I made it a point after that to make sure I learned the names of every member of my staff. When I would walk around my nursing center, I didn't want anyone to be surprised. He is a role model for me.

Harry is not a complicated man. He lives his life very gently. He could live in an expensive neighborhood but instead, he lives his life comfortably and honorably and takes enormous pleasure in the success of others.

What I have come to appreciate is his friendship. We get together for breakfast occasionally – meet at Famous Amos on University Boulevard and he orders two eggs over easy, toast, tea and bacon. He is not Kosher, but he is as Jewish a person as I've ever met. Harry embodies the 5th commandment – honor thy father and mother – he honored his parents and his wife. He is about kindness, decency and caring.

Beaver Street Fisheries is a remarkable company. Harry's still there every day. His routine serves him very well. His work ethic and his philanthropy go hand-in-hand. He helped us build our newest building at River Garden - The Frisch Pavilion for adult daycare. He's happy to take people there and tell them about it.

It's virtually impossible to say no to him if he asks you for something. He shared with me how he is at Mayo Clinic with the doctors there. So, I'm talking with him – telling him that River Garden is doing a lot of work with Mayo. He says, "Marty, would you like to meet the new president of Mayo – Dr. Gianrico Farrugia?" This was in September 2015. I said I would love to meet him and he said he would arrange it. Two days later, he's coming over for a tour of River Garden with the new president! They stayed for lunch.

I'm proud I made the Nomination for his OneJax Humanitarian Award. For a long time, Harry wouldn't allow anyone to honor him. He's very humble – doesn't seek fame or accolades. He does things because they are the right thing to do.

Harry is the real deal. Regardless of one's faith tradition, he and Lilo are what the religious leaders talk about when they reference someone who walks with their God. They took the gifts that were given them – gifts from God – and used them to the fullest to make life good for people. He's got hundreds of employees who depend on him, still – and they've never missed a paycheck. He has no debt. He treats everyone with respect – from a caregiver to a U.S. Senator – it doesn't matter – he treats everyone with respect and in turn, he gets it. You can't not love this guy.

Matt Schellenberg

I don't think Harry's ever met anybody he dislikes. As long as you're a good person, you're a friend of Harry's. He was more than a friend to me. He trusted me to go down to Orlando and represent him – he gave me that authority – what an honor it was to be able to speak for him. He's done it many times since then.

Harry and Shad Khan have a foundation to help young people transition from high school to college. It's an honor to be asked to look at the resumes and see the opportunity. I'm on the board with Lathun. Harry wants to help young people. It's his passion. He wants people to be the best they can be. We talk about everybody that applies – how our connections can help these people achieve their goals. There is so much generosity behind the scenes that people don't know about. I put in a resolution for Harry with the City of Jacksonville. It was well-deserved.

Dr. Floyd Willis, Frisch Family Physician – Mayo

Mr. Harry is one of the wisest people I've met in my life. I put maybe half a dozen people in that category – so wise that you really have to hang on to every word they say in case they say something that really will improve your life. His insights on dealing with people are really remarkable. I also think his insight on business is more remarkable than he even himself is aware.

An example of that is the conversation I had with him about fifteen years ago when we were in the midst of quite a bit of work – lots of meetings on improving patient care for all patients – quality improvement. Mr. Harry knew none of this, but he was talking about something that had happened in his office that was not to his liking and as he said something, I was taking it in. Something didn't go well at the office and here's my approach:

Dr. Floyd Willis and family, wife Wanda, daughter Joy and son Jackson

1. You have to find the problem.
2. What caused the problem.
3. You correct what caused the problem so that it never happens again.
4. Then you move on to the next inefficiency.

This was textbook quality process improvement that we do all the time at Mayo – I was simply amazed that he had been doing this way before it was written. It just proves that some people just get it. They have the skill – the insight – he probably never took a class on it. It was very interesting that he had that philosophy and approach. I didn't bore him – I simply asked him: Do you ever teach classes on stuff like this? Will you write a book on this?

Probably the only thing I feel matches his insight is his kindness and his deep desire to help someone if he can.

I've had situations as I've become his friend when I would have questions that go beyond doctor/patient relationship. My job is to be the professional, but they have been questions about situations that would prompt Harry to say, oh well, let me direct you to this person. Before I could get there, he will have taken the initiative to make it happen. I've had community questions – concerns about things that might be occurring, and he has connected me with people and impressed upon them the importance that he wants it to happen.

I've been at Mayo Clinic for 25 years, and I've been the Frisch family physician for that same period of time.

The words that come to mind when I think of Ms. Lilo are direct, kind-hearted, the consummate mother and grandmother – protective of everyone. I knew her as a patient and family friend for 25 years. She might tell you what she thought you needed to hear – 'You were late – I thought you had forgotten me!' She was direct. You needed to have a good answer for her. She was very smart and insightful. Ms. Lilo could have been a medical doctor. She knew about her family and their illnesses – about the human body and the human spirit. I made house calls for her. At certain times, I'd call and say I'm going to come by your house. It's a great gift for a patient. Harry and Lilo Frisch have been a great gift to me.

Dr. Steven Wallace – Former President of FCCJ (Now FSCJ)

Harry's personal story is one of the most compelling that I've ever heard – I met Harry about 20 years ago, back in 1997 when I first came to town as the new President of FCCJ. I realized early on that he really had an extraordinary personal story and family history. I love history. By now, I could tell his story almost as well as he can. We shot seven hours of video – I had that done – wanted it edited down to an hour at WJCT studios in Jacksonville. We had a number of plans – national distribution – I was former chair of WJCT board. If the Frisch family decides to go ahead with this video, I'm willing to produce it free of charge.

During my first four or five months here in town after I came to be President of FCCJ, I had a chance encounter with Harry at the University Club. He used to work out there – alternating between there and Epping Forest. He had just finished a workout. We talked for a few minutes and I told him I was brand new in Jacksonville, still just meeting people. He reached out to me shortly thereafter and invited me to lunch. He was so gracious – this speaks to his character and his love of our community.

Look at how he has built and maintained such extraordinary relationships with so many people. Harry is the most inclusive person I've ever met. He took an interest in this new guy and all it took was one lunch for us to become lifelong friends. I was absolutely enamored of the man. He is such a genuine,

Dr. Steven Wallace with wife, Amelia and son, Michael

authentic, caring individual who has achieved extraordinary things in his life. He's also incredibly humble. I was so inspired by him that we've had a close friendship ever since. We get together for lunch periodically and often go to events together.

He is one of my favorite people on the planet.

Harry invites the most diverse group of guests to his skybox. It's the most interesting group of people in the stadium – every time. He has both political parties represented, all sides of the political and social spectrum. Many public servants – CEO's – elected officials – very prestigious physicians and surgeons – some celebrities – you never know who you'll meet in Harry's skybox. Harry is so well-connected. It is a wonderful and fascinating experience to go to his skybox because, on any given day, the mix of people there is remarkable. I retired from the college at the end of 2012 and I'm currently doing some consulting work and some business entrepreneurial projects.

Here's a story about Wally Lee – he loved Harry and Harry thought the world of Wally. They had a great relationship, and I remember the way that got started. Wally retired as Chamber Chair in 2013 after 23 years as president and CEO of the Greater Jacksonville Chamber of Commerce. Harry and Wally did not know each other and that astonished me. I was amazed at what a low profile Beaver Street Fisheries maintained the community. There's no better success story – they just kept getting bigger, but their profile was not out there ... it's changed a little bit now and they've gotten involved with the chamber, but initially, there was very little if any involvement with the chamber. Harry has never been into self-promoting at all and has quietly done a phenomenal job. In all of my interaction with Harry I've discovered that his business philosophy is like the Harvard Business School perspective – all old school – he has rooted that business in the fundamentals and it has been incredibly consistent and disciplined. It really works. With all the innovations and modern trends, integrity and reliability still work best. Anyway, Wally and I had a conversation one day about what were the best businesses in Jacksonville – the highest performing

Wally Lee

and best-run businesses and I said I thought Beaver Street Fisheries was the best. Wally challenged that, saying "They are not prominent at all." I set up a lunch with Wally and Harry, and after about an hour and a half, as we were leaving the River Club, Wally turned to me and said, "You're right. They are the best run business in Jacksonville."

Wally had such admiration for Harry. Wally and I had planned on taking elements of that seven-hour video and having them separately edited into a shorter piece no more than 30 to 60 minutes in length for the Chamber, regarding Harry's business philosophy. He has established a truly phenomenal culture at Beaver Street. Sadly, Wally is gone now, but he did love Harry.

I'm amazed at the longevity of the employees at that company. It is not a cushy place to work. It is no nonsense, disciplined. I've heard that Harry has locked the doors for meetings that began at 8 a.m. and if you walk in one minute late, you're in trouble – the door might be locked.

David Stein - Philanthropist

I have always so admired his history – growing up in Austria with everything he could ever need to having to leave with nothing – from the penthouse to the outhouse! Coming here and building

Lilo, David Stein and Harry

the business they did – I've always been in awe. I met Harry 30 or 40 years ago. What he did was so amazing – to go from where he was to where he is now. I'm sure I've asked him for money – he's never turned me down.

Five points for giving money:
1. Really a good institution
2. Am I giving my time?
3. Am I giving my money?
4. Is the government paying for half of it?
5. What percentage is this of your income – figure it out.

It's all in the perspective.

The Frisch's are true history. Harry and I share mutual love and affection. Our relationship has been a #10 forever.

Chief Leonard Propper – JSO

I happen to live in the same condo on the beach where Harry has his condo, and he has been kind to my family. He owns a couple of garage spaces, one of which he shares with my wife and me, so she never has to get her hair wet in the rain. That kindness from him means a lot. I can't tell you how much we appreciate that. Harry has been so good to me, I want to make sure I do anything I can for him. If I had a call from Harry Frisch and a call from my wife, I'd call Harry back first. That's how much he means to me.

We first met at this restaurant called Two Doors Down. Harry always had a booth reserved there and anybody that was anybody and wanted to go into public office had to go through that booth. Me and my guys were just regular policemen – we didn't want anything from him. We'd go in and tease Harry … who are you eating with today? Whatever was going on in the city, you'd hear about it at Harry's table first – it was the Powerhouse booth and he entertained everybody from college presidents to council presidents! Everybody who was anybody made the rotation through that booth. I think he gravitated to us sometimes because we were just a bunch of guys – and we treated him like he was one of the guys.

In our lunch conversations with Harry, we'd always tell him, "If you need us, you'd better call." So, there was this one time when he was being recognized with an honorary degree from FSCJ and it was being presented to him at their graduation

Chief Leonard Propper & Harry Frisch

ceremony. Tammy Pate was taking him to the arena and traffic was a mess. She called me and said, "Leonard, we're in a bind. We're stuck in traffic and we have to be there in ten minutes. It turned out I was very close. I led them right to the front door *of the arena – right on time. It was a case of being at the right place at the right time and being able to do the right thing.*

My passion is the Police Athletic League and they have been a great support mechanism for me. I know in my heart that PAL makes a great difference in this community – and those guys holistically are very supportive of the Police Athletic League. They have never turned me down when I asked for something for PAL.

Nat Glover – Former Jacksonville Sheriff – Retired Edward Waters College President – Motivational Leader

Consistently and universally, Harry Frisch is the rare individual that you can't find anybody who will say anything bad about him. It is always complimentary, no matter who you are talking to – white or black – male or female – republican or democrat - and I can tell you, trying to navigate that political landscape and having a balanced persona is almost impossible, but he has managed to do that. Since Harry has been the benchmark, I've looked for others to try to measure up and sooner or later, if I found somebody

who I thought might come up to that status, then I later discovered that it was not the case. You'd either find some detractor or somebody who would have a different view, but Harry is the one who is tough enough to navigate through.

I could talk about his sensitivity to the community – so committed to helping kids in the inner city, regardless of color. I could talk about his insight and wisdom – how he taught me and helped me with my leadership style; how he taught me about sleeping on issues a couple of nights, and if they survive that, then maybe your decision will stand the test of scrutiny.

Harry is one of those people that you listen to and try to emulate. He validates you if you are a person who is trying to do the right thing for the right reasons. People do things differently and enjoy a certain level of success, but he is consistent and does the right thing for the right reasons – no matter what. He is one of my role models.

Congressman John Rutherford

I actually got to know Harry Frisch through being Sheriff in Duval County. He is such a community steward, like with the river taxi – he just went out and bought one and gave it to the city. He does amazing things like that for the city – and things like that for individuals, too. He has supported the Police Athletic League generously – a program that helps at-risk youth and builds a relationship between those youth and the police. It's a tremendous program and he's always supportive of that and also of the Justice Coalition. In the beginning, Harry was one of the biggest supporters of the Justice Coalition, which performs all sorts of wonderful tasks to take a lot of the pressure off of the Jacksonville Sheriff's Office.

As to my personal relationship with Harry, we have probably gone to lunch dozens of times over the years. He likes to set up regular lunches once a month or so. We haven't been able to since I left the Sheriff's office. Tammy would call and set it up and we'd meet for lunch. Ben or someone else would be there, like Lathun. We had the most memorable conversations about Harry's early life and how he immigrated to the U.S. – selling fish off a little wooden cart and building it into a multi-million-dollar business. It's an amazing story of entrepreneurship – a Horatio Alger story – and in the end, just giving back to everybody around him. It's always amazed me. When we went to lunch, I'd hear about what he'd just done at the gym – he is truly astounding.

Harry has been a dear friend for decades. He's a huge supporter of me which I particularly appreciate. You take what life gives you, but you don't give up. God honors you when you continue to give back. What is really great about this country is that we have individuals like Harry who give back so much because they know they've been blessed by God. When you travel through Europe, you don't find philanthropy like we have. It's only possible because of individuals like Harry Frisch. I fear we are losing that.

John Rutherford, David Stein, Admiral Kevin Delaney, Lathun Brigman, Harry Frisch, and Wally Lee

When Alexis de Tocqueville came to America, he said "America is great because America is good." He could have been talking about Harry. If America ever ceases to be good, she'll cease to be great. I fear we are losing some of that goodness because we are moving away from faith in our Judeo-Christian roots – like the Ten Commandments. Harry doesn't just talk faith, he lives it. To me, that's why he's such a great American.

Myron Flagler – CEO of the Jewish Community Alliance

I first met Harry and his wife Lilo about twenty years ago. They were so very supportive of all the things we've done at the JCA (Jewish Community Alliance). They particularly liked our cultural arts and speakers and Friday night programs. Harry and I quickly became fast and furious friends. Harry is a true friend. His friendship is unconditional – it is a gift. We still see each other almost monthly to have breakfast or lunch together and I

look forward to it. These are the things I love about Harry:

1. There is a Hebrew word – Tzedek – which, translated, means a very righteous person. Harry has always epitomized what a Tzedek is. He always did the right thing for the right reason and has an amazing humility around the things he has done and the untold countless people whose lives he has touched.

2. I lost my Dad at a relatively young age. My father came from the same part of Europe that Harry comes from and if I close my eyes, I can hear my Dad speak to me through Harry. Their voice and how they speak is so similar. It's sometimes eerie. Not only how they sound alike, but it's what he says. He gives me great insight with the life lessons he shares through his stories. He wrote this piece for business students at JU and once a year, I pass that list of Points of Good Business out to my staff and we review them together. They make so much sense. I ask the staff, "How is this applicable to what we do?" I remind them to remember Harry Frisch's rule –

two men on every job – sleep on something for two nights. It has helped us so much as an agency.

3. As the executive director of an agency, you don't often have people around you that can give you wisdom – sometimes it has to be self-generated. Harry is a reliable mentor. I ask his advice on things and he is always thoughtful in his answers. If he doesn't know, he will say he doesn't know and ask me to let him think about it.

An example of the great mentoring Harry has given me was when I told him this great idea I had to take my staff to Israel to ground us as an agency with our Jewish mission. I asked his advice on this and he said, "Myron, if you really want to do something special, study Israel with them for a year in advance – study the geography, history, economy, people – everything you can find about the country." We did this and my staff went to Israel with their eyes wide open – knowledgeable and able to understand what they were seeing. We've done that with every cohort we've taken to Israel, and it's all because of Harry's good advice.

Jeanine Rogozinski – President of the River Garden Foundation

Harry Frisch is the most benevolent and altruistic humanitarian I know. He is a paragon of Jewish values and wisdom – the touchstone of our Jewish community in Jacksonville. He has spent a lifetime building bridges and relationships and inspiring people of all ages. Harry is a role model and mentor for so many and Jacksonville is a better place because of his influence. He has truly inspired me to be a better person and a better volunteer.

Harry is a wonderful benefactor to River Garden and to just about every organization in Jacksonville. We are so lucky to have been the recipient of such a rare and brilliant man's generosity. He recognizes a need and is the first to step up and fill it. For many years, he would take no credit for his philanthropy. When I saw the word "anonymous" on a donation, I knew it was Harry Frisch.

Harry and Lilo were such a beautiful couple. They loved to dance. They used to belong to the Mr. and Mrs. Club at the Jacksonville Jewish Center. We recognized Harry and Lilo for their philanthropy at River Garden's 2012 Annual Gala. An example of Harry's commitment to River Garden ... on the Monday after the weekend of our annual Gala, he always calls the development office and reserves a table for the following year. He is an admirable, upstanding man – the kind of man you want your children to grow up to be.

Sam Rogozinski

My parents were immigrants. The Frisch's were among their closest friends when they got to the U.S. In fact, the Frisch family helped my parents become Americans, so I've literally known Harry Frisch my entire life.

After graduating from college, I worked for a bank in Atlanta for a while and then I went to Beaver Street and interviewed for a job with Harry. I went through the entire training program – driving trucks, forklifts, going out on deliveries, working in the accounting department, and I ended up working with Ben in the export division. I tell my kids and friends that I didn't have to get a Master's Degree – I got a Harry Frisch MBA. He is the most astute businessman I've ever known. We got to work at 7 a.m. and left at 7 p.m. and had a mandatory six-day work week, and having been trained that way, I don't know any different – I still work those hours!

The Rogozinski Family with Lilo and Harry on Ella Rogozinski's 80th birthday
L-R: Front Row: Jessica, Danielle, Dana, Erin and Laura
Center: Helen Pollan (Ella's sister), Ella, Lilo, Harry
Back: Sam, Randi, Abe, Marjie, Max, Zach, Jonathan, Josh Ben, Chaim, Jeanine

I worked at Beaver Street for ten years – from 1982 to 1992 and leaving there was a difficult transition to make. I truly loved working there. It was hard work and rewarding work – very fulfilling as well, but I had a chance to work with my family and Harry encouraged me to take that opportunity.

Harry has been a pillar of the community for so long. I remember, years ago when I was a child, knowing the Frisch family as some of the hardest working and sweetest, kindest people in Jacksonville. Harry's wife, Lilo, was a wonderful woman, may she rest in peace.

An example of how insightful Harry Frisch is as a businessman: We were buying product from a company that was going out of business and I ran into Harry's office and said, "Harry, this company's going out of business – let's make sure they don't owe us anything." He just smiled. He already had a check going to them, but he was holding it back to make sure they didn't owe us anything. He was way ahead of me. He always paid particular attention to details. I learned so much from him. Now, as Chief Operating Officer for Rogozinski Orthopedic Clinic, I try to emulate many of Harry's business practices.

John Peyton

Harry Frisch is a remarkable man who has inspired generations of leaders within his company and throughout our community. His principle-centered leadership, passion for his work and love for his family and coworkers has allowed Beaver Street Fisheries to experience tremendous success that has spanned multi-generations. Harry Frisch is an iconic business leader, community trustee, role model and, above all, good friend.

Former Mayor John Peyton, Harry Frisch and Senator Bill Nelson

Senator Bill Nelson

Harry is the embodiment of the American dream. From humble beginnings to business success, he never lost a personal humility and always gives back to his community and country. It is my honor to call him my friend.

Karen and Mack Mathis

My most vivid memories of Harry Frisch are those when he entered the Two Doors Down restaurant and everyone in the restaurant was happy to see him. Customers included the sheriff, police officers, judges, City Council members, state representatives, constitutional officers, the mayor, business owners, nonprofit leaders and neighbors. They all knew and

welcomed Harry and made sure to come by his reserved corner table to say hello. He knew them all and was genuinely pleased to see them. The mutual respect was a lesson for all of us.

Ilana Manasse

Our sages said: "Tov Shem tov, mishemen tov," meaning "It is better to have a good name than great wealth." Harry is very fortunate to have foremost a good name and a good heart, and then also great wealth. Harry is a man who is righteous and always willing to help. My late husband, Jack Manasse, worked with Harry and Fred at Beaver Street for many years. They have always been an important part of our lives.

Bob Simon, NOVA Fisheries, Inc., Seattle, Washington

My company of 30+ years has enjoyed great pleasure to work with Mr. Frisch and the many wonderful people at his company, Beaver Street Fisheries. I am certain there are many businesses who can attribute their business longevity to Mr. Frisch's example, just as our own company has benefitted. Each year I would come from Seattle to visit Beaver Street Fisheries, and each year Mr. Frisch took the time to sit with me and share his insight. In fact, for our company and many others - - so many of us are grateful beneficiaries of Mr. Frisch and his company. Beyond the many who work and have worked in Jacksonville at BSF over five decades, there are that many more of us around the United States and around the world who can attest to the good business sense and the shared goodness of Mr. Frisch.

Bob Simon's daughter, Samantha Simon (9) , finishing a dance with Harry at the wedding of Kimberly Troutman Shipley, daughter of David Troutman (BSF Team-Member) - 2004

Photo Gallery

Photo Gallery

Fred Frisch

Cornelia "Nellie" Frisch Rappaport

Harry Frisch in the lobby at Beaver Street Fisheries, Inc., posing with the American Flag and the elephant carved from one piece of rosewood (a gift to Harry of great honor from Ravi Chandler, a businessman from India). On the wall behind Harry are the formal portraits of the Frisch Brothers, Fred and Harry.

Ben and Karl

Ben, Lilo and Karl Frisch

Young Hans Frisch, businessman

Mark, Adam and Steven

Adam, Steven and Mark

Photo Gallery

L-R: Harry, Lilo, Erin, Daniel, Karl, Mark, Sierra, Steven, Meredith, Adam, Pat, and Ben

Photo Gallery

JCA Groundbreaking

Lilo and Steven Frisch

Harry and Fred

**Lilo and Jaguars
mascot Jaxon De Ville**

Another Groundbreaking!

Photo Gallery

David Troutman and Sam Kalil
2017 Boston Show

Food Support Team
2015 Greek Festival

Steven Frisch
2017 Boston Show

Ben Frisch, Jon Chaiton,
Glenn Pritchard
National Restaurant Show 2010

Photo Gallery

Karl and Lilo Frisch

Meredith and Mark

**Chaz Martin, Harry Frisch,
Lathun Brigman, Glenn Klauer**

**Over 20 years of service
Ms Kathleen and Family**

Jeff Mickler and family

Photo Gallery

**Over 20 years of service
Mr. Kelly Love and Family**

John O'Brien and Randy Helton

**Over 40 years of service
Darrell Glover & Terri Carrigg families**

Chaz Martin and Mark Frisch

Ben and Karl Frisch

Janet and Darrell Glover

Photo Gallery

Bill Gay and Harry Frisch

Bob Schircliff, Laurie DuBow, Mel Gottlieb, and Harry Frisch

Harry with Mayor and Mrs. Lenny Curry

Jeff Edwards and parents, Helene and Marvin Edwards

Gary and Nancy Chartrand and Linda and David Stein

Photo Gallery

**Eddie Norton, Britney Norton,
Missy and Karl Frisch**

Pat and Lyla ... swinging!

Ben and granddaughters ... boating!

Photo Gallery

Lilo at the beach!

**Standing: Ben, Pat, Erin, Adam, Sierra, Steven, Meredith, Mark, Missy, Karl, and Thora
Sitting: Lilo and Harry**

Photo Gallery

95th

**Celebrating Harry's 95th birthday
with his sons, Ben and Karl . . .**

**with his
granddaughter, Erin . . .**

and with his great-granddaughters, Hannah, Lyla and Abby!

Photo Gallery

David Long, Donnie Smith, Martha Barrett and Lathun Brigman

Birthday celebration at BSF! Cake courtesy of the Jacksonville Jaguars!

Mike Gvozdich and John Geer

Jeff Edwards, Bob Shircliff, Kerri Stewart, Bill Gay, Harry, and Cleve Warren, FSCJ Foundation Executive Director

Nat Glover, Virginia Norton and Mack Mathis

Gail and Mike Balanky

L'CHAIM! TO LIFE!

CHAPTER FOURTEEN: Reflections on Life

You get back what you dish out. Values are not negotiable. Punctuality means respect. You need to set an example by being on time. You need to count pennies and dollars. One dollar starts out with a penny. The wisdom of our American forefathers is shown in the money that says, "In God We Trust." Be humble. Believe in God in Heaven. I know God created us.

I'm not a religious man, but I probably believe more in God than most people you meet. My Jewish religion is in me. I inherited my religion from my parents and grandparents and ancestors. It was good for them and it's good for me.

My belief in God is bigger than religion. When Lilo was sick, there were health people here 24/7. Listening to some of those people, I'm sure God created us. Only God could have created women to be the same wherever they live and whatever race they are – it is by the grace of God that women all go through the same exact cycles of living, and that they can reproduce with a man and bear children. Only God could have come up with that plan. It is by the grace of God that all humans can share their blood, depending on their blood-type, but that the same blood runs through all of us. Only God could do that.

Nobody's got the right not to respect God's Ten Commandments. They are not requests ... they are God's orders. This country was built on the Ten Commandments and the rule of God. Church and state cannot be separated.

Respect is important. I respect everybody's religion. Tammy in my office is Christian and I would never begin a meal without allowing her to say grace. Nat Glover (former Jacksonville Sheriff, now retired President of Edward Waters College) told me that I'm the only person he knows who is friends with everyone – no matter what party they belong to, what color they are, or what religion they are. Lathun Brigman is a deacon in the First Baptist Church downtown. He is one of my best friends in the world.

I have no enemies that I know of. There is nothing in the world that I cannot put my name on. I've never done anything underhanded. I've worked hard to be the best because there is no room for second best in my mind. Because I've worked so hard, I've gained a lot of respect. For instance, if somebody wants to talk with Senator Bill Nelson, I just say to my assistant, Tammy, please call Bill Nelson. He's a friend of mine.

Love is good. I know that love is good. I was married to Lilo for 68 wonderful years, and we never went to bed angry.

John Butler at Walmart sent me an email when he retired. He said that people come into your life for a reason, a season or a lifetime, and he said that he would be my friend for a lifetime. It touched me when he said that.

On July 5, 2018, I was 95 years old. God is keeping me healthy. I feel that God is directing me to do what I need to do to keep healthy – speaking to me and putting thoughts in my head. For instance, I was a smoker for years. I smoked Winston cigarettes – two packs or more a day - and had a huge inventory of cigarettes in our warehouse. I could get them tax-free from the Carolinas and the Navy base. I had no intention of quitting. Then, I had a disappointing checkup conversation with our family dermatologist, Dr. Kartsonis. He told me, "I keep telling you to quit smoking and you keep smoking. If you're not listening to me and following my advice, I can't be your doctor anymore." He was going to fire me as his patient. That hurt my feelings.

Soon after Dr. Kartsonis said that to me, I was driving to the office and saw the big billboards along the way – "WINSTON TASTES GOOD LIKE A CIGARETTE SHOULD." "MARLBORO COUNTRY." I began to get mad when I saw those billboards and I thought, "I'm no sucker for anybody!"

Then, later that day I was sitting in my office and in my mind, I saw a big fat guy with a pink-looking face and a sarcastic smile. He had a big cigar in his mouth. In my mind, he was Chairman of the Board for Winston Cigarettes. He smiled that sarcastic smile and said, "Dummy, I got you."

NO! Nobody got me! I quit smoking right then. It's the same way with chocolate. I don't want to be a diabetic. Thora monitors my blood sugar every single morning. If my blood sugar is high, I cut it out that day. I have respect for my God … when I hear that little voice in my head that says, "No more chocolate today," I listen.

It's a pleasure to be healthy enough to go into my office every day. It's also a pleasure to be able to handle business with one phone call. On a recent day, I enjoyed two interesting phone calls. Former Mayor Jake

Godbold called to tell me he was celebrating his birthday on December 14, 2017 and he wanted me to sit at the head table at River City Brewing Company. The second call was from Senator Aaron Bean, asking me to sponsor a fund raiser for the best kept secret in Jacksonville, UF Shands Hospital, on February 3, 2018, at the Hyatt Regency Hotel. It gives me such satisfaction to know that people like these respect me enough to invite me to sit at their table.

Recently, my oldest great-granddaughter, Lyla, had a birthday and I asked their mother, Meredith, to bring Lyla and her sisters, Hannah and Abby to come to visit me. Thora had presents wrapped for all three girls and we enjoyed a special afternoon together. Spending time with those precious little girls meant the world to me.

When our grandchildren came along, Lilo and I would often take the family out to dinner at Famous Amos – never any fancy places – just good, reasonably priced food. I still like to sit at the breakfast table at Famous Amos sometimes

Meredith, Lyla, Hannah, Papa Harry and Abby

with my friends David Stein, Myron Flagler and Marty Goetz. To some degree, being Jewish is a burden I share with them. Jews have always been the scapegoat – even back to Biblical times when we were the slaves of the Pharaohs – not for love or money will that ever happen to us again! Never again! That's what we said over and over when I lived in Palestine. Family and friends are what life is all about.

What people don't understand is that a college degree might give you a great education – you might even end up brilliant – but college doesn't teach people to know what they don't know. I've had high-priced consultants come into my office at Beaver Street and ask me what my secret to success is – I tell them I've learned to USE MY HEAD because I only had a 7th grade education. Using my head is my secret – that's what Lilo always told me – Use Your Head. She raised our sons to use their heads, too. She gave them good backbone for later in life. Both boys worked at the fish market and both of them attended military school to learn discipline – there were no privileges unless they used their heads – if they didn't behave, they got demerits. Lilo gave them her heart and soul – she gave them discipline and love.

- *Health and happiness are not for sale.*
- *God gave us a brain and we need to use it.*
- *There is no grey zone between right and wrong. There is only fog in the middle.*
- *When I'm working, I'm relaxing.*
- *You can only eat with one spoon at a time.*

You do the things in life you need to do. There's a little voice in my head that says, "Harry, you need to do this ... or you don't need to do this."

I told Jacksonville Sheriff Mike Williams, "You won't solve the problems by putting more policemen on the streets. You'll just give the shooters more targets. Put the Ten Commandments in every home. Teach the children to respect the Ten Commandments. Even a little baby knows right from wrong. Be a role model – model the commands of God."

Use Your Head

"May you live until 120" is a Jewish blessing. I started this book when I was 94 – until 120. The age of Moses upon his death is said to have been 120, but the most important thing about this age was that the Bible states, "his eye had not dimmed, and his vigor had not diminished." (Deuteronomy 34:7). My eyes can still see – not as well, but well enough … and my vigor remains strong. I still climb 25 steep steps to and from my office every day of the week and am planning my retirement party from Beaver Street Fisheries on my 100th birthday, July 5th, 2023. It will be at Epping Forest Yacht Club … finally, a day off!

My son, Ben, calls me every night. No matter what, he takes the time to call me. He is a busy man and will probably never retire … just like me, he loves to work. He is, in my opinion, one of the best businessmen in the country.

My son, Karl, is now retired and makes himself available to me whenever I need help. I usually see him on Sundays, or more often if needed. During the last hurricane, I stayed at his big house in Mandarin. He is a good man. Karl gives me the Yiddish Calendar every year and I love some of the ancient sayings … they are still true today:

> **Voil tsu dem mentshen vos baglikt oif der elter.**
> Fortunate is the man who has a happy old age.

> **Gadles ligt oifen mist.**
> Pride lies atop the dung heap.

> **Der ponem zogt ois dem sod.**
> The face tells the secret.

> **Az me hot nisht tsu entferen, muz men farshveigen.**
> If you don't have anything to answer, it's best to keep quiet.

Gebentsht zenen di hent vos tuen zich alain.
Blessed are the hands that will do things themselves.

Durch shveigen ken men nisht shteigen.
You can't get ahead by keeping quiet.

Es libt zich alain, shemt zich alain.
He who praises himself will be humiliated.

Dos gantser leben iz a milchomeh.
All of life is a struggle.

A patsh fargait, a vort bashtait.
A slap may pass, but the word remains.

Ven a ganef kusht, darf men zich di tsain ibertsailen.
When a thief kisses you, count your teeth.

Az me shport nisht dem groshen, hot men nisht dem rubel.
If you don't save the penny, you won't have the dollar.

Az me laigt arein kadoches, nemt men arois a krenk.
Invest in a fever and you'll realize a disease.

Dos voremel nart op, un nisht der fisher oder di vendkeh.
It's the bait that lures, not the fisherman or the tackle.

Der man iz der balbos – az di veib zeineh lozt.
The husband is the boss – if his wife allows.

Fun a prosteh bulbeh kumt arois di geshmaksteh latkeh.
From the humble potato you get the tastiest pancake.

Ain mitzvah bakumt anander.
One good deed leads to another.

Az me gait gleich, falt men nisht.
If you walk straight, you won't stumble.

Mentsch tracht, Got lacht.
Man plans, God laughs.

Mit honik ken men chapen mer fligen vi mit essik.
With honey you can catch more flies than with vinegar.

Der grester shvimmer kon zich dertrunken.
Even the best swimmer can drown. (Even experts make mistakes).

Oplaigen iz nor gut for kez ober nisht far a chaseneh.
Delay is good for cheese, but not for a wedding.

Fun krimeh shiduchim kumen arois gleicheh kinder.
From bad matches good children are also born.

Der emes kumt arois azoy vi boimel oif der vasser.
Truth rises to the surface like oil on water.

Di vos vaksen nisht, veren klainer.
Those who do not grow, grow smaller.

Besser a vaitik in harts aider a charpeh in ponem.
Better a pain in your heart than shame before men.

A shverer beitel macht a leicht gemit.
A heavy purse makes a light spirit.

Gan'aiden un gehenem ken men baideh hoben oif der velt.

Heaven and hell can both be had in this world.

Ven dos mazel kumt, shtel im a shtul.

When fortune comes calling, offer him a seat.

Naches fun kinder iz mer tei-er far gelt.

Joy from children is more precious than money.

Iz er a gever? Zol er kreien!

Is he a rooster? Let him crow!

Oib me git dir, nem; oib me nemt fun dir, shrei gevald!

If someone gives to you, take; but if they take from you, scream!

Shver iz nor dem ershten mol.

The hardest thing is the first step.

Mit geduld shept men ois a k'val.

With patience you can drain a brook.

Vos bashert dos vert.

What is meant to be will be.

Host du, halt; vaist du, shveig; kens du, tu!

If you have, hold on to it; if you know, be silent; if you can, do!

I have this quote from Pastor Martin Niemoller
on the wall in my conference room at home.
It is true and we need to remember it
so that what happened in the Holocaust
will never happen again:

" First they came for the socialists,
and I did not speak out—because I
was not a socialist.

Then they came for the trade
unionists, and I did not speak out—
because I was not a trade unionist.

Then they came for the Jews,
and I did not speak out—because I
was not a Jew.

Then they came for me—and
there was no one left to speak for me."

Pastor Martin Niemoller

The Ten Commandments are
God's answer to
all the woes of this world.
I just wish we could live by them.

THE TEN COMMANDMENTS

I. Thou shalt have no other Gods before me

II. Thou shalt not make unto thee
any graven image

III. Thou shalt not take the name
of the Lord thy God in vain

IV. Remember the sabbath day, to keep it holy

V. Honor thy father and thy mother

VI. Thou shalt not kill

VII. Thou shalt not commit adultery

VIII. Thou shalt not steal

IX. Thou shalt not bear false witness
against thy neighbor

X. Thou shalt not covet

Exodus 20

Biographer's Note:

Photo by Dr. Edward M. Lee

Writing this book about Harry Frisch has been a privilege and an adventure! Harry is one of the wisest men I've ever known. He is loved and respected by so many who wanted to pay tribute to him that this book could have become the size of an old-fashioned city phonebook! It finally became clear to me that the only way to get this memoir completed was to let everyone have their say and simply arrange their eloquent quotes in some semblance of order. I hope you enjoy reading this history of an incredible man as seen through the eyes of so many who love him ... including me!

Respectfully,
Susan D. Brandenburg